SIT BACK, RELAX, AND ENJOY THIS COLLECTION OF UNIQUE BUFFALO RECIPES

BUFFALO SPREE

The Magazine of Western New York

Food for Four Seasons

ISBN: 978-0-9895640-0-7

Published by Buffalo Spree Publishing, Inc.
100 Corporate Parkway, Suite #220
Buffalo, NY 14226
716-783-9119 \ buffalospree.com

Edited by Christa Glennie Seychew
Photography by Melissa and Nino Ocampo
Creative direction by Chastity Taber
Design by Catherine Sollenberger

A portion of the proceeds from the sale of this book will be donated
to the SPCA Serving Erie County.

Printed in the United States of America

INTRODUCTION

Western New York is rich in independently owned restaurants, especially given our size and demographics. It is clear that we—particularly those of us who live within Buffalo's metro area—love to eat. We are blessed with a rich, blue collar history that has rendered old school pub food like wings, hot dogs, beef on 'weck, and bologna sandwiches so common that they act, in some ways, as examples of our community identity. Today there are more pub-style restaurants in WNY than any other sort. Typically operated by families, these eateries have served homey, hearty food in large portions ever since they were first imagined as places for workaday folk to find sustenance at lunch or after a shift.

But over the last twenty years, dining has changed—across the country, and in WNY. We now have a wide assortment of fine dining restaurants, more sushi spots than we know what to do with, capable and unassuming Asian restaurants typically operated by immigrants, and perhaps—most importantly—a growing number of restaurants owned and operated by chefs themselves. These chefs, committed to sourcing the best ingredients they can find, have turned to farmers and local markets in order to incorporate the fruits, vegetables, and meat raised in our region.

Despite having published recipes from chefs and restaurants in its pages for many years, *Buffalo Spree* has never published a cookbook. Since I began writing about food in 2006, the Western New York dining scene has dramatically evolved, and looking forward, it doesn't appear to be slowing a bit. So what better time than now to record where we are in WNY's ever-changing food history?

Spree's publisher, Larry Levite, and I set out to publish a cookbook that showcases all of our restaurants, from family-friendly pubs to establishments that offer luxurious fine dining, and *Food for Four Seasons* is just that. No restaurant was charged to participate; no chef or owner paid fees of any kind. Instead, a general letter went out to every restaurant we could think of, requesting that they assist us in documenting this moment in WNY's restaurant history. Within these pages, you'll find chefs and over fifty-six restaurants spanning from Chautauqua to Niagara Falls.

It is a joy to work so closely with those who spend their lives cooking and serving others, and *Food for Four Seasons* is dedicated to the many people who make WNY's thriving independent restaurant scene hum. We hope this book finds a place among your favorite cookbooks and that each time you look at it you are reminded of our region's talented food growers and chefs, and the amazing bounty they provide for us, both in the fields and on restaurant menus.

Eat local!

Christa Glennie Seychew
Senior Editor/Food Editor, *Buffalo Spree*

CONTENTS

RECIPES FROM BUFFALO'S RESTAURANTS

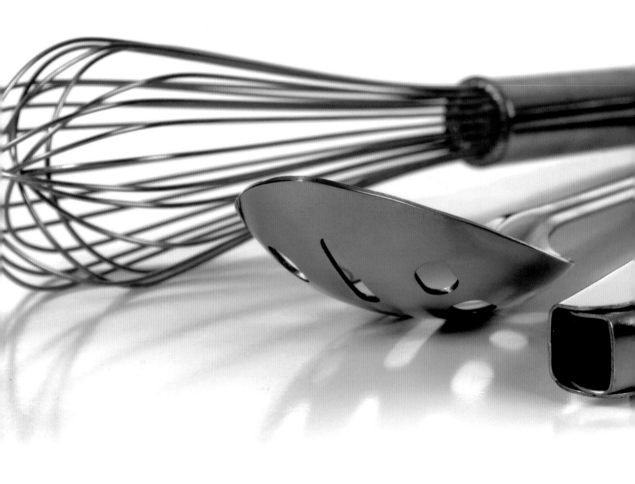

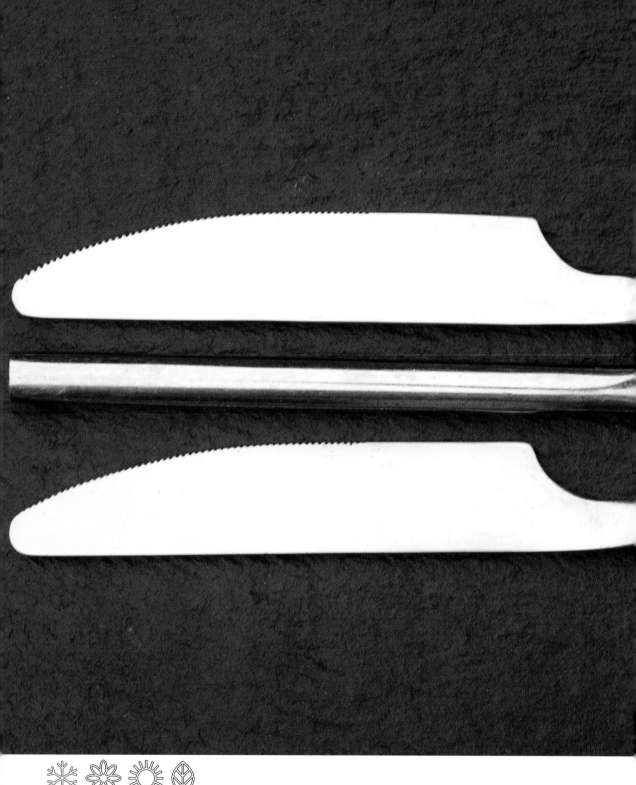

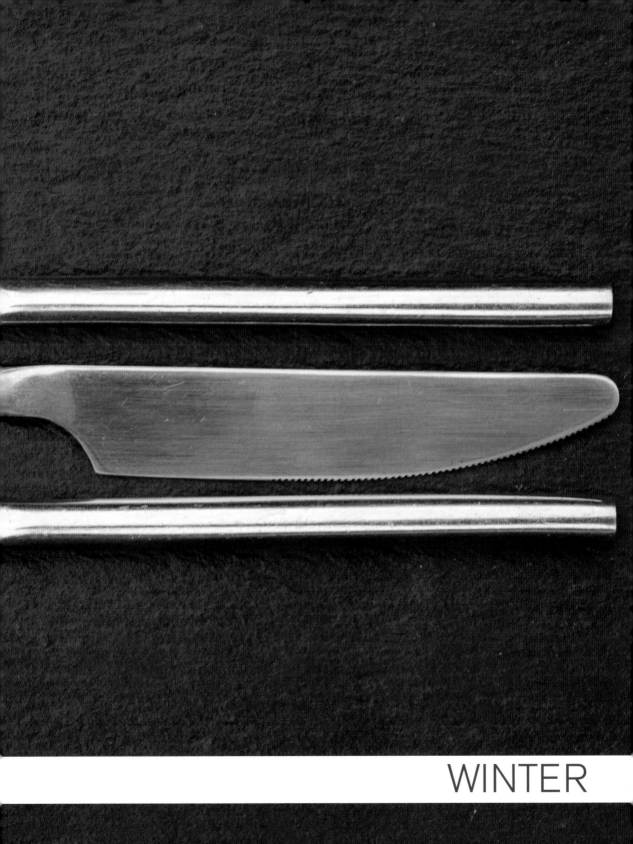

WINTER

Plum Gin Gimlet

BREEN SHEA, TRATTORIA AROMA

YIELDS 1 DRINK

ROSEMARY FOAM*

4 cups hot water

1 bundle fresh rosemary

5 gelatin sheets

Ice water

Pinch of salt

Pinch of sugar

In a mixing bowl, steep rosemary in hot water for 10 minutes. While rosemary is steeping, bloom gelatin sheets in ice water for 5 minutes. Once they are soft, squeeze gelatin sheets, removing excess water. Strain water, discarding rosemary. Add sugar and salt to season. Whisk in bloomed gelatin until dissolved, and cool. Pour liquid into iSi whipper and double charge.

PLUM GIN GIMLET

2 ounces Averell Plum Gin

1/2 ounce Falernum syrup

1/2 ounce freshly squeezed lime juice

Add all ingredients to a cocktail shaker and dry shake for 10 seconds. Add ice and shake for an additional 10 seconds. Fill a rocks glass with ice and strain the cocktail into the glass. Shake loaded iSi whipper vigorously for 10 seconds and dispense foam onto cocktail.

*If you do not have access to an iSi whipper, skip the foam recipe and simply muddle a sprig of fresh rosemary in the bottom of your cocktail shaker before adding the mixture. Falernum can be found in gourmet shops in the cocktail mixer section.

Chicken and Chevre Wonton Ravioli

LUIGI ALFANO, THE HOLLOW BISTRO AND BREW

SERVES 12

2 boiled chicken breasts, finely chopped

1 cup Chevre cheese

5 fresh basil leaves, chopped

1/2 teaspoon garlic, chopped

2 large eggs

1/2 cup Parmesan, grated

Salt and white pepper, to taste

1 tablespoon heavy cream

1 package wonton wrappers

In a large mixing bowl, combine chicken, Chevre, basil, garlic, 1 egg, parmesan, salt, and pepper. Mix thoroughly using your hands. In a separate bowl, make an egg wash by combining the remaining egg with cream. Whisk.
Working on a flat surface, place 1 teaspoon of the chicken mixture in the center of each wonton. Paint a thin line of egg wash around all 4 edges of each wrapper. Top with another wonton and seal by gently pressing all edges closed with the tines of a fork. To cook, place raviolis in gently boiling water for about 5 minutes and serve with your favorite marinara or cream sauce.

Spicy Banana Pepper Dip

COLIN CAVE, THE EAGLE HOUSE RESTAURANT

SERVES 10

5 banana peppers, roughly chopped

1 large red bell pepper, cleaned and chopped

1 small bunch scallions, cleaned and chopped

1 tablespoon red pepper flakes

2 8-ounce packages cream cheese, softened

1/2 cup Gorgonzola, crumbled

1/2 cup Asiago, grated

1/4 cup Parmesan, grated

1/4 cup unseasoned breadcrumbs

Preheat oven to 350 degrees. Soften banana peppers by boiling in just enough water to cover. Drain. Once cool, add to a food processor, along with red bell pepper and scallions. Pulse until combined. Add red pepper flakes and half cream cheese and blend again. Add Gorgonzola and remaining cream cheese and blend until smooth. Pour mixture into a large mixing bowl. Add 1/4 cup asiago and all the Parmesan cheese and breadcrumbs to the bowl and mix by hand until combined. Place mixture in a casserole dish and bake in the oven for 12 to 15 minutes. Two or three minutes before the dip is done, sprinkle remaining Asiago on the top and return to the oven to brown. Serve with crostini, tortilla chips, or toasted pita.

Loaded Baked Potato Bisque

LUIGI ALFANO, THE HOLLOW BISTRO AND BREW

SERVES 6

1/2 cup vegetable oil

1 1/2 cups bacon, chopped

1 medium white onion, chopped

1/2 celery stalk, chopped

8 large Idaho potatoes, peeled and chopped

1 large carrot, chopped

8 cups water

8 cups heavy cream

Salt and white pepper to taste

2 cups sharp Cheddar, grated

1/4 cup scallions, sliced

ROUX

1 tablespoon unsalted butter, cold

1 tablespoon all-purpose flour

Place oil and bacon in a large pot and cook over low heat for 7 minutes. Add onion, celery, potatoes, and carrots and continue to cook for another 7 minutes. Add water and increase heat to high, cooking until all vegetables are tender. Reduce heat to medium high and add heavy cream. Bring to a boil and simmer for 10 minutes. Add salt and pepper to taste.

Purée ingredients with a hand blender. Add Cheddar and stir until melted. If the soup is a too thin, use the roux.

To make the roux, combine the butter with flour and mix thoroughly. Bring the pot back to medium heat. Return the soup to the pot and whisk in the roux. Stirring regularly, cook for another 15 minutes until desired thickness has been reached. Garnish with scallions.

Porcini Mushroom Bisque

BRIAN MIETUS, BACCHUS

SERVES 10

1/4 cup extra virgin olive oil

2 cups celery, chopped

2 cups onion, chopped

2 tablespoons garlic, chopped, plus 1 teaspoon garlic, minced

2 cups fresh cremini mushrooms

2 cups dried porcini mushrooms

1 cup tomato, diced

1 bunch fresh thyme, stems removed

2 cups arborio rice

2 cups dry white wine

8 cups chicken stock

2 cups heavy cream

3 bay leaves

1 cup fresh shiitake mushrooms

1 cup oyster mushrooms

Salt and pepper, to taste

1/2 cup Parmesan, shaved

6 tablespoons truffle oil

Heat half the olive oil in a large stock pot. Add celery, onions, chopped garlic, and 1 cup of cremini mushrooms and sauté until soft. Add the dried porcini, tomato, three-quarters of the thyme, and the rice. Season with salt and pepper and continue to cook over medium heat for 3 to 5 minutes. Add wine and reduce by half. Add the chicken stock, cream, and bay leaves and bring to a boil. Reduce heat and let simmer, stirring occasionally for 45 minutes. Preheat oven to 425 degrees. While soup is cooking, prepare remaining mushrooms for the garnish. Trim the stems and toss with remaining olive oil and thyme, minced garlic, salt, and pepper. Place on a baking sheet and roast for 15 minutes. Remove from oven and set aside to cool.

When the soup is finished, blend with a hand blender and run through a fine-mesh strainer or chinois. Add salt and pepper to taste. To serve, garnish with the roasted mushrooms, Parmesan, and truffle oil.

BRIAN MIETUS, EXECUTIVE CHEF/OWNER, BACCHUS

His career began at the sink, washing dishes at his mother's hot dog stand, but twenty-five years later, Mietus has had quite a career, earning accolades from *Wine Spectator*, two James Beard dinners, and fawning reviews from critics for the fine fare and excellent service delivered at his downtown restaurant, Bacchus.

What is your favorite kitchen tool?

"A juicer. Most people use it for healthy living, but we use it to make cocktails and sauces mounted with butter or olive oil."

Porcini Mushroom Bisque from Bacchus

Buffalo Chicken Mac 'n' Cheese

JILL FORSTER, NICKEL CITY CHEESE AND MERCANTILE

SERVES 4

4 boneless skinless chicken thighs

2 teaspoons kosher salt

2 teaspoons black pepper

2 tablespoons vegetable oil

1/3 cup Frank's Red Hot Pepper Sauce

1/2 cup Mountain Gorgonzola, crumbled

1 pound cavatappi pasta

3 tablespoons unsalted butter

3 tablespoons all-purpose flour

1 pound Cabot Clothbound Cheddar, grated

2 1/2 cups whole milk

Salt, to taste

Preheat oven to 375 degrees. Place the chicken thighs in a mixing bowl. Add salt, pepper, oil, and 2 tablespoons of the hot pepper sauce. Mix to coat the thighs evenly. Place thighs on a roasting rack with a sheet pan underneath to catch drips. Roast for 35 to 45 minutes, or until cooked through. Cool to the touch and cut into bite-size cubes.

Using a container with a leak-proof lid, add the remaining hot sauce and the chicken pieces. Cover and toss firmly, coating the chicken. Refrigerate for at least 30 minutes.

Cook the pasta according to package directions, but only for two-thirds of the recommended cooking time. Chill in ice water to stop the cooking. Strain and refrigerate until ready to use.

In a large, heavy sauce pot, melt the butter and add the flour, making a roux. Whisk the roux over medium heat for 5 minutes. Remove the pot from the heat, and slowly add the milk, stirring constantly. Return the pot to medium heat and bring to a simmer, stirring frequently for 15 minutes. Add the Gorgonzola and

Cheddar in thirds while stirring constantly. Bring to a simmer before adding the next batch of cheese. When finished adding the cheese, add salt to taste.

Add the pasta to the cheese sauce and mix well. Add the cubed chicken thighs and combine. Simmer for 5 minutes, or until everything is well heated.

Honey and Spice Roasted Carrots and Parsnips

JOE GEORGE, 20TH CENTURY CLUB

SERVES 8

4 medium carrots, peeled and sliced into 1-inch pieces

4 medium parsnips, peeled and sliced into 1-inch pieces

1/4 cup olive oil

2 teaspoons honey

1 teaspoon salt

1 teaspoon chili powder

1/2 teaspoon ground cumin

1/4 teaspoon ground cinnamon

1/4 teaspoon ground allspice

1/8 teaspoon ground cayenne pepper

Preheat oven to 400 degrees. Combine all ingredients in a medium bowl and toss thoroughly, coating the vegetables with the seasonings and oil. Allow the carrots and parsnips to marinate for 30 minutes at room temperature.

Heat a large nonstick skillet over high heat and add the seasoned vegetables. Sauté and toss the vegetables for 5 minutes, or until they begin to caramelize. Transfer the vegetables to a medium roasting pan and roast in the oven for approximately 25 minutes, or until they are nicely browned and cooked throughout. Serve warm or at room temperature.

Potatoes au Gratin with Beer and Jarlsberg Cheese

JOE GEORGE, 20TH CENTURY CLUB

SERVES 10

2 pounds potatoes, washed and sliced 1/4-inch thick

2 cups beer

1 bunch scallions, sliced thin

1 teaspoon kosher salt

1/2 teaspoon black pepper

1 teaspoon chili powder

1 teaspoon ground cumin

1 teaspoon garlic, minced

1/2 cup fresh basil, chiffonade

2 large eggs

2 cups Jarlsberg, shredded

Preheat oven to 350 degrees. Combine the potatoes and beer in a medium pot and bring the beer to a boil over medium-high heat. Reduce the heat to low, and simmer for approximately 10 minutes. Drain the potatoes, reserving the liquid (there should be approximately 1 cup of liquid remaining); allow the liquid to cool to room temperature.

Once the liquid has cooled, combine it in a large bowl with the scallions, salt, pepper, chili powder, cumin, garlic, basil, and eggs. Whisk mixture together until thoroughly combined. Add the cooked potatoes and cheese; gently toss together. Transfer the potato mixture to a lightly greased casserole dish. Bake for 30 to 45 minutes, or until the custard is set and the surface is golden brown.

Eggplant Parmesan

LOU BILLITTIER, JR., CHEF'S

4 SERVINGS

1 large eggplant

1 tablespoon dried oregano

1 cup Parmesan, grated

1 tablespoon parsley, chopped

3 cups breadcrumbs

1 cup all-purpose flour

3 eggs, beaten

1 1/2 cups olive oil

1 jar Chef's Restaurant Plain Pasta Sauce

Salt and pepper, to taste

1 cup low-moisture Mozzarella, grated

Peel the eggplant and slice into 1/4-inch lengths. Combine the oregano, 1 tablespoon Parmesan, salt, pepper, and parsley with breadcrumbs. Create a breading station by putting the flour, eggs, and breadcrumbs into three separate shallow dishes. Dredge each slice of eggplant in the flour first, then the beaten egg, followed by the breadcrumb mixture. Rest the slices on a baking sheet until ready to cook.

Heat the olive oil in a frying pan. Add eggplant slices carefully. Cook for about 3 minutes on each side, or until light brown. Remove and drain on paper towels.

Preheat the oven broiler.

Heat the pasta sauce in a saucepan. Using an ungreased casserole dish, place the eggplant in a single layer along the bottom of the dish. Ladle some of the pasta sauce over the top and sprinkle with the remaining Parmesan and Mozzarella cheese. Bake the eggplant about 5 minutes under the broiler until the cheese begins to brown.

Ristorante Lombardo's Braised Oxtail with Horseradish Gremolata

MICHAEL OBARKA, EXECUTIVE CHEF, RISTORANTE LOMBARDO

Entirely self-taught, Obarka delivers scratch-made Italian fare at Lombardo's, the venerable, yet modern Hertel Avenue restaurant he's worked at since 2007, winning the hearts and palates of guests, new and old, one bite at a time.

What do you consider the most exciting aspect of Buffalo's dining scene?

"Customers are showing an increasing willingness to try something a little different. Slowly but surely, we're breaking down walls in this town."

Braised Oxtail with Horseradish Gremolata and Semolina Gnocchi

MICHAEL OBARKA, RISTORANTE LOMBARDO

SERVES 6

OXTAIL AND RAGU

- 5 pounds oxtail (thicker end, preferably uncut)
- 2 medium onions, diced
- 2 large carrots, diced
- 4 stalks celery, diced
- 8 garlic cloves, thinly sliced
- 4 cups red wine
- 2 cups canned San Marzano tomatoes, crushed by hand
- 6 anchovy fillets
- 2 cups veal stock
- 2 tablespoons fresh thyme, stems removed
- 2 sprigs rosemary, stems removed
- 1 tablespoon fresh marjoram, stems removed
- Salt and pepper, to taste

Preheat oven to 350 degrees. In a Dutch oven, brown the oxtail evenly on all sides until golden brown. Transfer the oxtail to a plate or baking sheet. Set aside. Add the onion, carrot, celery, and garlic to the pan and sauté until lightly browned. Add the wine to the vegetables and stir until the fond (all of the brown bits on the bottom of the pan) dissolves. Place meat back into the Dutch oven. Add the tomatoes, anchovies, stock, and herbs to the pot. The liquid should leave the meat uncovered by one-third. If more is required, add a little stock. Cover and cook in the oven for 2 1/2 to 3 hours, or until meat pulls from the bones. Remove the meat, bones, and fat from the pot, holding the meat to the side. Discard the bones and fat. Stir the remaining ragu thoroughly. Return the warm meat to the pot. Season with salt and pepper.

SEMOLINA GNOCCHI

- 3 cups milk
- 1/3 cup unsalted butter, preferably European
- Salt and pepper, to taste
- 1 cup semolina flour
- 4 egg yolks
- 1/2 cup Parmesan, grated
- 1/2 cup Pecorino Romano, grated

Preheat oven to 425 degrees. Place milk, butter, a couple pinches of salt, and a couple grinds of black pepper into a medium saucepan, and gently bring to a boil. Whisk the semolina in, pouring it in a slow, thin stream so that no lumps form. Switch to a wooden spoon and stir vigorously until thick, about 2 to 3 minutes. Remove pan from the heat and add one egg yolk at a time until completely incorporated. Spread the mixture onto a baking sheet, and let the gnocchi dough cool and firm up. Cut into desired shapes and place in an ovenproof dish. Top the gnocchi with the oxtail ragu and bake at 425 degrees until ragu is bubbly and the gnocchi edges are golden brown. Garnish with more Parmesan and Horseradish Gremolata.

HORSERADISH GREMOLATA

- 2 tablespoons horseradish, grated
- 2 tablespoons flat-leaf parsley, finely chopped
- Zest of two lemons

Combine ingredients in a small bowl. Hold until ready to garnish.

Crispy Duck Breast with Pear and Walnut Stuffing in a Green Peppercorn Sauce

ANDREW NUERNBERGER, THE ROYCROFT INN

SERVES 4

PEAR AND WALNUT STUFFING

- 1 Bartlett pear, peeled and diced
- 4 tablespoons walnuts, crushed
- 4 tablespoons unsalted butter
- 1 tablespoon unseasoned breadcrumbs

Heat butter in a pan over medium heat. Sauté the pear and walnuts until warmed through and slightly caramelized. Be careful not to burn the walnuts. Add breadcrumbs and mix to bind. Set aside and keep warm.

DUCK

- 4 duck breasts, cleaned and trimmed
- Salt, to taste

Heat a heavy skillet over high heat. Pat the duck breasts dry with a paper towel and season with salt. Place the breasts skin side down in the skillet. Reduce heat to medium. Cook 10 minutes, or until skin is crisp and mahogany colored, removing fat from the pan as it is rendered. Turn breasts and cook until finished. Set aside and keep warm.

GREEN PEPPERCORN SAUCE

- 1/4 cup apple cider
- 1/2 teaspoon cornstarch
- 1 tablespoon Calvados apple brandy (or brandy)
- 1 tablespoon green peppercorns, drained and crushed
- 2 tablespoons duck demi-glace (substitute store-bought demi if homemade is unavailable)
- 1 sprig fresh thyme, stems removed

Combine apple cider and cornstarch, creating a slurry. In a small saucepan, heat brandy, peppercorns, demi-glace, and thyme. Bring to a simmer. Slowly add slurry, using a whisk to combine until a sauce-like consistency is achieved.

To serve, slice a pocket in each duck breast and insert stuffing. Pool green peppercorn sauce on the bottom of the plate and top with stuffed duck breast. Serve with wild rice or acorn squash.

Braised Short Rib Pasta

ANDREW MURTHA, BRICK OVEN BISTRO AND DELI

SERVES 6

4 tablespoons vegetable
oil

6 pounds boneless beef
short ribs, cleaned and
trimmed

Kosher salt

3 carrots, peeled and
chopped

1 leek, chopped

2 medium onions, chopped

1 bulb garlic, crushed

1/4 cup tomato paste

1 bouquet garni (sachet) of
fresh thyme, fresh bay
leaf, and peppercorn

1 cup dry red wine

1 pint chocolate stout

2 quarts veal stock

1 quart mushroom broth

Preheat oven to 375 degrees. Heat oil in a large pot on the stovetop over high heat. Season the beef with salt and add to pot. Sear the beef on all sides. Remove the beef from the pot and let rest. Drain the oil from the pot and return it to the stove over medium-low heat. Add the carrots, leek, onion, and garlic and cook until the onions become translucent. Add the tomato paste and cook until the vegetables begin to caramelize. Deglaze the pan with the wine and beer. Reduce heat and simmer for 10 minutes, cooking off the alcohol. Add the veal stock and mushroom broth. Bring broth up to a simmer and return the short ribs to the pot. Cover and braise over low heat for 4 to 6 hours.

Once the meat is tender and falling from the bone, remove from the braising liquid and set aside. Strain the braising liquid through cheesecloth or a fine-mesh sieve. Return liquid to the pan and allow to rest so that any fat can be skimmed from the top.

Place the beef and braising liquid in a sauté pan. Use a spoon or ladle to take liquid from the bottom of the pan and pour it over the beef repeatedly, until the beef is coated with the stock and becomes glossy.

PASTA

2 tablespoons unsalted
butter

1 tablespoon shallot,
minced

1 teaspoon garlic, minced

1/2 cup sherry wine

3/4 cup mushroom broth

1/4 cup heavy cream

Salt, to taste

2 tablespoons chives,
chopped

2 tablespoons parsley,
chopped

1 pound fresh pappardelle
pasta, cooked according
to package instructions

Heat a large sauté pan over medium heat. Add 1 tablespoon of the butter, followed by shallot and garlic. Sweat the garlic and shallot, but do not brown them. Add the wine, and reduce by half. Add the mushroom broth, and again reduce the sauce until it develops a dark, rich consistency. Add the cream and stir thoroughly until combined. Add remaining butter, herbs, and pasta. Toss. Add salt to taste.

Plate the pasta and top with the glazed beef.

Southern Shepherds Pie

ADAM ZIMPFER, FAT BOB'S SMOKEHOUSE

SERVES 6

1/3 cup vegetable oil

1/2 cup all-purpose flour

1/2 cup onion, diced

1/2 cup carrot, diced

1/2 cup sweet potato, diced

1/2 cup celery, diced

1/2 cup red bell pepper, diced

1 jalapeño, seeded and minced

1/2 cup black-eyed peas, cooked

1/2 cup fresh corn

1 tablespoon fresh garlic, minced

3/4 pound smoked beef brisket, chopped
  (or ground beef)

3/4 cup andouille sausage, diced

4 cups chicken stock

2 teaspoons ham base or concentrated bouillon

1/3 teaspoon dried thyme

1/3 teaspoon dried marjoram

1/3 teaspoon dried sage

1/3 teaspoon ground black pepper

1/3 teaspoon salt

6 cups mashed potatoes

1 cup bacon, cooked and crumbled

Preheat oven to 350 degrees.

Add oil to a sauté pan over very low heat. Gradually sprinkle the flour into the hot oil and stir. Cook, stirring mixture constantly, forming a roux. Continue to cook 12 to 15 minutes until roux has taken on a warm brown color. Remove from the heat and continue stirring until the roux has cooled and there's no risk of burning. Set aside.

In a Dutch oven, cook the onion, carrot, sweet potato, celery, peppers, peas, and corn until vegetables are about halfway done. Add meat. If using ground beef, cook through. In a separate sauté pan, fully cook the andouille sausage. Add the sausage to the large pot of vegetables. Add the chicken stock, ham base or bouillon, and seasonings. Simmer until vegetables are tender. Bring pot to a boil and add the roux one third at a time. Combine thoroughly and return to a boil. Repeat this process until desired thickness has been achieved.

In a large baking dish or individual crocks, add hot pie filling. Top with potatoes and bacon. Heat in oven until pie filling is bubbling.

Lamb Bolognese

CONOR CASEY, COCO

SERVES 6

2 tablespoons vegetable oil

2 1/2 pounds ground lamb

1 medium onion, chopped

2 carrots, chopped

1/2 bunch celery, chopped

4 cups dry red wine

1 bay leaf

1 sprig rosemary, stems removed

1 sprig fresh thyme, stems removed

2 tablespoons ground cinnamon

1 cup heavy cream

Salt and pepper, to taste

6 cups pappardelle pasta, cooked

Parmesan cheese, grated

Heat oil over medium heat in a large Dutch oven or heavy-bottomed stock pot. Add lamb and brown. Remove from the pot and hold to the side. Cook onion, carrots, and celery until translucent. Add the red wine and herbs. Increase heat and bring to a boil. Lower heat and reduce liquid by one-third. Add the cinnamon and cream. Stir to combine. Return lamb to pan and continue to simmer until flavors are well combined. Serve over pasta and top with grated cheese.

Peppered Beef Stew

KARL WYANT, VERA

SERVES 6

2 pounds tenderloin tips, cubed
4 tablespoons vegetable oil
1 1/2 cups celery, chopped
1 1/2 cups carrots, chopped
1 1/2 cups onion, chopped
1/4 cup garlic, thinly sliced
2 cups dry red wine
1/4 cup granulated sugar
4 28-ounce cans of whole, peeled tomatoes
1 tablespoon ground black pepper
Salt, to taste
2 tablespoons fresh rosemary, stems removed and chopped
1 tablespoon fresh oregano, stems removed and chopped
Pecorino Romano, grated

Season meat with salt and pepper. In a 6-quart stock pot, heat 2 tablespoons of the vegetable oil over medium heat. Add beef and brown on all sides, cooking each side 4 to 5 minutes. Remove meat from pan and hold in the refrigerator. Add remaining oil to the pot and cook celery, carrots, onion, and garlic until they begin to brown. Add the wine and sugar and continue to simmer over medium heat for approximately 5 minutes. In a large bowl, crush each of the tomatoes by hand, reserving juices. Add the tomatoes and their juice to the stock pot. Add black pepper and herbs and cook for 90 minutes. Return beef to the pan and cook 10 to 15 minutes until the beef is warmed through. Season with salt and pepper to taste. Garnish with cheese and serve.

Pan-seared Wild Striped Bass with Chive Spaetzle, Roasted Vegetables, and Mustard Pancetta Vinaigrette

CHRISTOPHER DAIGLER, ENCORE

SERVES 4

MUSTARD PANCETTA VINAIGRETTE
1/2 pound pancetta, diced
2 tablespoons Dijon mustard
1 tablespoon whole grain mustard
3 tablespoons champagne vinegar
2 tablespoons fresh chives, chopped
2 tablespoons fresh shallots, chopped
1 cup extra virgin olive oil
1 tablespoon sea salt
1 tablespoon white pepper
1 tablespoon fresh thyme

Cook pancetta in a sauté pan over medium heat. Allow it to brown evenly. Reserve all rendered fat. In a blender, combine pancetta, rendered fat, mustards, vinegar, chives, shallots, and seasonings. Pour in the olive oil in a stream, blending until smooth. Check seasoning and set aside.

WILD STRIPED BASS
4 8-ounce portions of wild striped bass, skin on
2 tablespoons sea salt
1 tablespoon white pepper
1/4 cup Wondra flour
2 tablespoons vegetable oil
1 tablespoon olive oil

Preheat oven to 450 degrees. Season bass with

salt and pepper and dredge in Wondra flour. Heat a large ovenproof sauté pan over medium heat. Add oils. Place fish skin side down. Cook for 1 to 2 minutes, until fish skin is golden brown and crispy. Flip the fish over and repeat. Move pan to the oven and cook for 8 to 10 minutes. (Accompanying mushrooms and fennel can be roasted in the oven with the fish simultaneously.)

CHIVE SPAETZLE

- 4 cups water
- 1/2 pound fresh chives
- 1 cup milk
- 3 cups all-purpose flour
- 1 tablespoon sea salt
- 1/2 tablespoon white pepper
- 2 tablespoons olive oil

In a large saucepan bring water to a boil. Prepare an ice bath for blanching. Drop the chives into the boiling water for 10 seconds, then move them to the ice bath.

In a saucepot, bring the milk to a gentle boil. Once the milk is warm, add the chives and remove from the heat. Place milk and chive mix into a blender and puree until the chives are completely liquefied and infused into the milk. Place the flour, salt, and pepper in a large mixing bowl. Add the chive milk and, using a wooden spoon, mix until combined. As the dough gathers into a ball, scrape excess flour from the sides of the bowl. Cover in plastic wrap and place in refrigerator to chill for a minimum of 20 minutes. Bring a pot of salted water to a boil. Using a spaetzle maker* coated lightly with oil, add the spaetzle mix to the boiling water and cook until the dumplings float to the top. Immediately remove the spaetzle and strain. Add the two tablespoons of olive oil to a medium-sized mixing bowl. Toss spaetzle gently in the bowl to prevent them from sticking. Reserve in the refrigerator until ready for use.

*If you do not have access to a spaetzle maker, the dough can be rolled by hand. Place a dime-sized piece of the pasta in your hand and rub your hands together, rolling an oblong shape. Cook according to directions listed above.

ROASTED MUSHROOMS AND FENNEL

- 3 tablespoons olive oil
- Salt and pepper, to taste
- 1 cup shiitake mushrooms, julienned
- 1 fennel bulb, quartered

Preheat oven to 450 degrees. Add olive oil and salt and pepper to a mixing bowl. Toss the mushrooms and fennel. Roast on a baking sheet, removing the mushrooms after 6 to 8 minutes. The fennel may require 10 to12 minutes to soften and become golden brown. Slice fennel prior to serving.

ASSEMBLE

Reheat the spaetzle in a sauté pan with olive oil. When it becomes crisp and the edges begin to brown, add the roasted vegetables and heat through. Portion spaetzle out onto four plates. Top with fish and dribble with vinaigrette.

Sausage and Greens

MICHAEL SINATRA, SINATRA'S

SERVES 6

6 links Italian sausage,
   sweet or hot

4 tablespoons olive oil

3 heads escarole

2 cloves garlic, chopped

Pinch of red pepper flakes

Salt and pepper, to taste

4 tablespoons Asiago,
   grated

Bring a pot of water to boil on the stovetop.

Cut each sausage link into four pieces. Heat 1 tablespoon of the olive oil in a separate pan over medium-high heat. Add sausage and cook until done. Remove from pan and set aside.

Wash escarole thoroughly. Cut each head in half. Blanch in boiling water for 2 minutes. Drain and hold.

In the the pan used to cook the sausage, add remaining olive oil, garlic, and red pepper flakes. Sauté until warm and fragrant. Return the sausage to the pan and add the drained escarole. Cook for 2 to 5 minutes until all is warmed through. Season with salt and pepper to taste.

Divide into six portions and top with the Asiago.

Ma-Po Tofu

2-2, KAYDARA NOODLE BAR

SERVES 6

PORK AND STOCK

- 4 cups water
- 1 pork tenderloin, cleaned and trimmed (12–16 ounces)
- 1 bunch scallions, roughly chopped
- 5 tablespoons fresh ginger, peeled and minced
- 2 ribs celery, minced
- 3 kaffir leaves (bay leaves may be substituted)
- 1 medium ripe tomato, quartered
- 3 star anise

In a large pot, combine water, pork tenderloin, half of the scallions, the ginger, celery, kaffir leaves, tomato, and star anise. Bring to a boil over medium heat and simmer for 90 to 100 minutes until pork is tender. Remove pork. Once cooled, cube and hold in refrigerator. Meanwhile, using a fine-mesh strainer, strain the remaining liquid into a pot and cook with the lid off until reduced to approximately one cup. Set aside.

TOFU AND SAUCE

- 1 block of silken tofu, firm
- 1 egg
- 1 tablespoon ginger, peeled and minced
- 3 cloves garlic, minced
- 1/2 teaspoon ground white pepper
- 1 tablespoon oyster sauce
- 1 tablespoon soy sauce
- 1 tablespoon fish sauce
- 1 tablespoon mirin
- 1 tablespoon cornstarch
- 1 teaspoon granulated sugar

Prepare the tofu by first draining it, and then resting it on a paper towel for 10 minutes. Cube and set aside. Combine all the remaining ingredients in a bowl. Add tofu, coating thoroughly. Cover and allow to marinate for 45 minutes.

PREPARE

- 2 bunches scallions, trimmed to 1/2" length, green and white parts separated
- 1/4 cup mirin
- 6 bundles cooked somen noodles, nested, kept at room temperature
- 1 tablespoon gojuchang (Korean pepper paste) or more, to taste
- 1–6 hot peppers, cleaned and chopped (optional)
- 1 head garlic, minced

In a large, hot sauté pan, char the green portion of the scallions. Remove from pan and set aside on a paper towel. Reheat the pan, add the white portion of the scallions, and repeat char. Use the mirin to deglaze the pan. Add half the stock and simmer. Season with the marinade, adding as much or as little as you like. Add cubed cooked pork and a tablespoon of gojuchang. If the sauce is too thick, add more broth. Gently fold in tofu and the charred green scallions. Serve over somen noodle nests. Garnish with chopped hot peppers.

Cornmeal Encrusted Monkfish with Winter Squash Hash and Brown Butter Sauce

CRAIG MOORE, GRANDSTANDS BAR AND GRILL

SERVES 4

- 3 cups yellow cornmeal
- 8 4-ounce monkfish medallions (substitution: skinless haddock or cod)
- 3 tablespoons olive oil
- 1 medium shallot, sliced

2 cloves fresh garlic, chopped

1 sweet potato, peeled, 1/2-inch dice

2 1/2 cups butternut squash, peeled, 1/2-inch dice

1 1/2 cups fresh pumpkin, peeled, 1/2 inch-dice

1/4 cup apple cider (or juice)

1 1/2 cups chicken stock

4 sprigs fresh thyme, stems removed

Salt and pepper, to taste

1/4 cup vegetable oil

1 1/2 cups salted butter

4 fresh sage leaves, chiffonade

4 fresh sage leaves, whole

Preheat oven to 375 degrees. Place cornmeal in a shallow dish. Place each fish medallion in cornmeal, pressing down when necessary to adhere cornmeal thoroughly. Set the fish aside. Heat a large sauté pan to medium high. Add the olive oil. When the oil is hot, add the shallot and cook until translucent. Add the garlic and cook until it becomes fragrant and begins to brown. Add the sweet potato and butternut squash and cook on medium heat for 5 minutes, stirring frequently. If the oil is absorbed while the ingredients are still cooking, add more, a little at a time. Add the pumpkin and continue to cook for another 2 minutes.

While the hash is still cooking, begin to cook the fish by heating a large cast-iron or nonstick sauté pan to medium-high heat. Add three-quarters of the vegetable oil. Once the oil is hot, add half the monkfish being careful not to overcrowd the pan. Once the first side of the fish is golden brown, flip and allow the other side to brown. When the second side is golden brown, remove the fish and place on a paper towel to absorb any excess oil. Place the fish on a lightly sprayed sheet tray and put in the oven to finish, about 8 minutes. Briefly return to the hash, adding the apple cider, 1 cup of the stock, the thyme, salt, and pepper. Reduce heat to a low simmer. Stirring occasionally, cook until the hash is fork tender and the liquid is absorbed. If still a little underdone, add the remaining stock and continue to simmer until tender.

Remove hash from the heat, cover, and set aside. For the brown butter sauce, in a small pan, slowly melt the butter and bring up to a low simmer, stirring frequently. After a few minutes the milk solids will begin to brown and take on a nutty aroma. When this happens, remove from heat and add the fresh sage. Continue to stir until all the bubbling stops.

To plate, scoop the winter squash hash onto the center of the plate and place two pieces of fish on top. Top with the brown butter sauce and garnish each plate with a fresh sage leaf.

Almond Crescents

TRISH MULLANEY, DESSERT DELI GOURMET BAKERY AND CAFE

YIELDS 3 DOZEN COOKIES

DOUGH

1/2 pound blanched almond meal, toasted

1 1/4 cups granulated sugar

2 pounds unsalted butter

3 cups all-purpose flour

1 teaspoon salt

SUGAR MIXTURE

2 cups granulated sugar

2 teaspoons cinnamon

Preheat oven to 325 degrees.
Combine almond meal, sugar, and butter in a mixing bowl. Using an electric mixer, beat until light and fluffy. Add flour and salt and continue to beat until incorporated. Gather 2 tablespoons of dough from the bowl and shape into a crescent. Repeat, lining cookies on an ungreased cookie sheet.
Bake for 20 to 25 minutes.
Remove from oven and allow to cool slightly. Roll cookies in sugar mixture.

German Chocolate Cake

DEBORAH CLARK, DELISH

YIELDS ONE 8-INCH CAKE

FILLING

- 1 1/2 cups heavy cream
- 1 1/2 cups granulated sugar
- 3/4 cup unsalted butter, room temperature
- 5 eggs, yolks only
- 2 cups pecans, toasted and chopped
- 2 cups coconut, toasted
- 1 1/2 tablespoons vanilla extract

Combine cream, sugar, butter, and yolks in a heavy-bottomed saucepan over medium-high heat. Stir constantly until the mixture comes to a full boil. Reduce heat to medium and let soft boil for 4 to 5 minutes. Meanwhile, in a mixing bowl, add pecans, coconut, and extract. Set aside.

As soon as the yolk mixture has become thick and deep yellow in color, remove it from the heat and immediately pour it over the bowl filled with nuts and coconut. Stir to blend, and allow it to sit at room temperature for 1 hour. Refrigerate the filling mixture for a minimum of 3 hours.

CAKE

- 4 cups unbleached all-purpose flour
- 2 teaspoons baking soda
- 1 cup unsweetened cocoa
- 1 cup unsalted butter, room temperature
- 2 cups granulated sugar
- 2 large eggs
- 2 teaspoons vanilla extract
- 1 cup sour cream
- 1 cup hot water

Preheat oven to 350 degrees. Lightly butter 3 8-inch round cake pans. Line with parchment paper, and lightly butter and flour the paper (or spray with an unflavored pan-release spray).

In a mixing bowl, combine flour, baking soda, and cocoa. In a separate bowl, use a handmixer to beat the butter until it is pale yellow and fluffy. Add the sugar, and continue mixing until combined. Then, one at a time, add the eggs, mixing until they are thoroughly incorporated. Add the vanilla and mix again.

Add the dry ingredients to the creamed butter mixture in thirds, alternating with the sour cream and the hot water, beginning and ending with the dry ingredients.

Divide the batter between the prepared pans, and tap the pans once, on the counter, settling the batter. Bake in the center of the oven until the cakes are puffed and spring back when lightly touched, 35 to 40 minutes.

Remove the cakes from the oven and transfer to a wire rack to cool. When they are cool, turn them out of the baking pans, fill, and frost.

DEBORAH CLARK, OWNER, DELISH

Deborah Clark's cooking school and pastry shop has long been a popular stop for aspiring cooks and those with a sweet tooth. Having won several awards for its coffee, cookies, cakes, and classes, Delish is an important fixture in Buffalo's emerging Black Rock neighborhood.

What is your favorite kitchen tool?

"A heat-proof rubber spatula. It's like an extension of my arm when I'm baking."

GANACHE

1 1/2 cups heavy cream
1 pound semisweet or
    bittersweet dark chocolate,
    chopped

In a heavy saucepan, heat cream until just before it begins to boil. Turn off the heat. Add chopped chocolate and let it rest, untouched, until melted. Use a rubber spatula or whisk to stir the mixture until all the pieces are melted. Pour it into a room-temperature bowl and let it cool to room temperature until it is thickened but still pourable. Cover leftover ganache with plastic wrap and refrigerate. Reheat in the microwave or over a double boiler and use for a topping for ice cream or to drizzle on other desserts.

ASSEMBLE

1/4 cup pecans, toasted and
    chopped
1/4 cup coconut, toasted

Bring the filling back to room temperature before layering cake. Filling should be soft enough to easily spread on cooled cake layers. If making multiple layers, divide filling accordingly. Spread filling between layers. Finish the cake with a generous glazing of ganache, chopped pecans, and toasted coconut. Refrigerate for at least 3 hours or overnight. Bring back to room temperature for 30 minutes before serving.

Chocolate Banana Cake with Brown Butter Frosting

ROSS WARHOL, ATHENAEUM HOTEL

YIELDS ONE 8-INCH CAKE

CAKE

- 2 cups granulated sugar
- 1 3/4 cup all-purpose flour
- 3/4 cup Dutch-process cocoa powder
- 1 1/2 teaspoons baking powder
- 1 1/2 teaspoons baking soda
- 1/2 teaspoon salt
- 2 large eggs
- 1 cup ripe banana, mashed
- 1 cup warm water
- 1/2 cup buttermilk
- 1/2 cup canola oil
- 1 1/2 teaspoons vanilla extract

Preheat oven to 350 degrees. In a medium bowl, whisk together the sugar, flour, cocoa powder, baking powder, baking soda, and salt. In a large bowl (or the bowl of a stand mixer), add eggs, banana, water, buttermilk, oil, and vanilla. Beat on medium speed until combined. Slowly add the dry ingredients to the wet ingredients, mixing until thoroughly combined. Grease and flour 2 8-inch cake pans, tapping out excess flour. Pour the batter into the prepared cake pans and bake for 35 to 40 minutes, or until a cake tester comes out clean. Let cake cool on racks.

FROSTING

- 1 1/2 cups unsalted butter
- 4 1/2 cups confectioners sugar, sifted
- 2 to 3 tablespoons whole milk

Melt butter in a sauce pan over low heat. Allow the butter to brown, cooking slowly until it becomes amber in color and has a nutty aroma.

Transfer butter to a small bowl and cool in refrigerator until it becomes solid, but is still soft enough to cream with remaining ingredients. Add butter and powdered sugar to a mixing bowl (or the bowl of a stand mixer) and cream together on low speed. Add the milk until desired consistency is reached.

ASSEMBLE

Remove the cakes from the pan. Place 1 cake on a plate and frost only its top. Place the second over it and frost the top and sides of the double layer cake. Leave finished frosted cake at room temperature.

Chocolate Stout Pie

CYNTHIA RICHERT, TORCHES

YIELDS ONE 9-INCH PIE

CRUST

- 1 1/2 cups all-purpose flour
- 1 teaspoon salt
- 3 tablespoons granulated sugar
- 3/4 cup unsalted butter, cold and cubed
- 4 tablespoons cream cheese
- 2 tablespoons cold water, more or less

In a large mixing bowl, combine flour, salt, and sugar. Cut in butter and combine until it resembles coarse meal. Cut in cream cheese. Sprinkle cold water over this mixture gradually, and mix just until the dough holds together, being careful not to overwork the dough. Gather into a disc and wrap in plastic wrap. Refrigerate for a minimum of 30 minutes. Gently turn the dough out onto a floured board. Roll out into a circle large enough to fill your pie pan; the dough will be about 1/4-inch thick. Place into a greased 9-inch pie pan. Chill in the refrigerator while preparing the filling.

FILLING

- 3 eggs
- 1 cup light brown sugar
- 1 teaspoon vanilla extract
- 1 cup light corn syrup
- 2 tablespoons unsalted butter, melted
- 1/4 cup stout beer
- 2 cups pecans, chopped
- 3/4 cup semisweet chocolate chips

Preheat oven to 375 degrees.

In a mixing bowl combine the eggs, sugar, vanilla, corn syrup, butter, and stout. Mix until smooth. Place chopped pecans and chips into chilled pie crust. Cover with sugar and stout mixture.

Bake for 15 minutes, then turn the oven temperature down to 350 degrees and bake until the center of the pie has risen, approximately 30 minutes.

SPRING

Pork or Shrimp Shumai

MIKE ANDRZEJEWSKI, SEABAR

PORK FILLING

MAKES APPROXIMATELY 20
PIECES

- 1 pound ground pork
- 2 tablespoons garlic, minced
- 1 tablespoon fresh ginger, grated
- 1 jalapeño, minced
- 2 tablespoons soy sauce
- 1 egg
- 1/2 cup scallion greens, chopped
- Sriracha Hot Chili Sauce, to taste
- 2 tablespoons granulated sugar
- Ground black pepper, to taste

Add pork and all remaining ingredients to a large mixing bowl. Be sure to add fresh pepper and chili sauce in small amounts, depending on how much heat you want. Gently combine all ingredients, mixing until well blended.

SHRIMP FILLING

MAKES APPROXIMATELY 32
PIECES

- 1 pound shrimp, peeled
- 1 egg white
- 1 tablespoon fresh ginger, grated
- 1 tablespoon fish sauce
- 1 tablespoon granulated sugar
- Sriracha Hot Chili Sauce, to taste
- 1/2 cup scallion greens, chopped
- 1/8 cup cilantro, chopped

Place peeled shrimp in a food processor and pulse until mostly smooth. Add sugar, ginger, fish sauce, and chili sauce, and pulse until well blended. Transfer to a mixing bowl and blend in scallion and cilantro.

MIKE ANDRZEJEWSKI, EXECUTIVE CHEF/OWNER, SEABAR, CANTINA LOCO, MIKE A @ HOTEL LAFAYETTE, TAPPO

Long recognized as Buffalo's "celebrity chef," Andrzejewski is best known for his unique take on Asian fusion cuisine, but in recent years this James Beard "Best Chef" finalist (2008, 2010) has branched out, adding four innovative, food-driven restaurants to his resume.

DIPPING SAUCE

- 1/2 cup soy sauce
- 1/4 cup rice vinegar
- 1 tablespoon brown sugar
- 1 teaspoon garlic, minced
- 1 teaspoon fresh ginger, minced
- 1 tablespoon barbecue sauce or ketchup
- Sriracha Hot Chili Sauce, to taste

Place all ingredients in a mixing bowl. Whisk until combined. Hold aside until shuimai are ready to eat.

Pork or Shrimp Shumai

ASSEMBLE

1 package prepared
  wonton wrappers,
  approximately
  48 wrappers*
Egg yolk, beaten

Place 6 wonton wrappers on a work surface, scoop 1 1/2 tablespoons of either filling in center of wrapper and fold edges to form a cup, open at the top. Repeat until filling is used entirely. To cook, steam in an Asian style stovetop steamer or place a little oil in a pan, heat over medium heat until hot. Add shumai (open top up) and lightly brown bottom. Very carefully pour in about a 1/4 inch of water (be careful, oil will pop and sputter) and cover. Steam until water evaporates and shumai begin to sizzle. Check for doneness; add a little more water, if needed, to cook longer. Serve with dipping sauce.

* Please note, each filling recipe makes a different number of dumplings. The number of wrappers you will need is based on whether or not you make both fillings or just one.

Bellweather Cocktail

TOMMY LOMBARDO, RISTORANTE LOMBARDO

YIELDS 1 DRINK

1 ounce cucumber-infused gin*
1 ounce Dolin Blanc vermouth
1/2 ounce Creme de Violette
1/2 ounce freshly squeezed lemon juice
Fresh sprig of lavender (garnish)

Combine ingredients in a shaker glass or tin. Add ice, shake vigorously, and strain into a chilled martini glass or coupe. Garnish with a fresh sprig of lavender.
*Cucumber gins are available, but you can also make your own by combining 2 seedless cucumbers that have been peeled and grated with one liter of gin. Refrigerate the cucumber and gin mixture, allowing it to steep for 3 days. Pour it through a fine strainer or chinois before serving. Store extra gin in the refrigerator.

Sautéed Sea Scallops with Crispy Pancetta, Shiitake, Wilted Radicchio, and Chive Butter

DANIEL JOHENGHEN, DANIEL'S RESTAURANT

SERVES 4

4 tablespoons olive oil
1/2 cup pancetta, diced
8 shiitake mushroom caps, halved
16 large sea scallops, dry packed
4 large heads radicchio, halved

1/2 cup dry white wine
1/2 cup unsalted butter
4 tablespoons chives, chopped

Heat olive oil in a medium sauté pan. Add pancetta, mushrooms, and scallops. While scallops are searing, stir pancetta and mushrooms until crisp. Remove pancetta and mushrooms, set aside, and keep warm. When seared on one side (approximately 2 minutes), turn scallops over and add radicchio to the pan. Continue cooking until radicchio is wilted and scallops are golden brown. Remove from pan and set aside.
Add the wine to the pan, scraping the fond (browned pieces on the bottom of the pan) free. Cook until the wine is reduced by half. Slowly whisk in butter until emulsified and add chives. To serve, place radicchio in center of plate and top with scallops. Arrange pancetta and mushrooms around the scallops. Pour sauce over scallops and serve.

Spring Pea Bisque

EDWARD FORSTER, THE WORKSHOP

SERVES 10

SOUP

3 tablespoons olive oil
1 large onion, diced
6 cloves garlic, peeled
1/2 large bulb fennel, diced
Salt and pepper, to taste
5 cups peas, blanched and shocked
1 cup spinach, firmly packed
6 cups milk
6 cups water
1/8 teaspoon xanthan gum
1 tablespoon extra virgin olive oil

GARNISH

1 cup peas, blanched, shocked, double shucked (garnish)

1 cup sunflower seeds, toasted

Salt, to taste

Olive oil, as needed

Optional garnish ingredients: fresh pea leaves,
    freeze-dried peas

Heat olive oil in a large pot over low heat. Add
the onion, garlic, and fennel and sweat until
tender. Season with salt and pepper. Increase
temperature to high heat and add peas until
warm. Add spinach, and cook until the leaves
wilt. Season with salt and pepper. Pour onto
a parchment-lined sheet tray and chill in
refrigerator immediately.

Once chilled, transfer to a large blender or food
processor in batches, depending on the size of
your equipment, scaling batched ingredients as
necessary. On high speed, purée peas with equal
parts milk and water. Once contents are blended
smooth, dust the xanthan gum into the blender
vortex. Blend 5 seconds, then add the tablespoon
of olive oil. Season with salt and pepper. Pass
through chinois or a fine-mesh strainer. Chill until
ready to use.

CHAMOMILE FROMAGE BLANC

1 tea bag of ground chamomile flowers, bag
    discarded

1 cup Fromage Blanc

1 tablespoon honey

Salt, to taste

Combine tea and fromage blanc in a mixing bowl.
Add honey and season with salt.

POACHED EGG

10 eggs

Find instructions for poaching eggs on page 115.
possible. Hold warm until all eggs are cooked.

PREPARE

Heat soup. Season garnish with salt and olive oil.
Arrange garnish in the bottom of each soup bowl,
creating a nest that the egg can rest on. Place egg
atop pea/sunflower/pea leaves, season with coarse
salt. Pour soup into bowl gently. Garnish with
fromage blanc.

Sautéed Asparagus with Poached Egg and Truffle Oil

PAULA DANILOWICZ, THE FILLING STATION

SERVES 4

1/2 cup white wine vinegar

24 stalks fresh asparagus

1 tablespoon unsalted butter

Salt and pepper

4 large eggs, poached

8 tablespoons white truffle oil

1/4 cup Parmesan, freshly grated

Bring a small sauce pan of water to a boil, reduce to a simmer and add the vinegar. Trim asparagus and quickly blanch. Using tongs, gently remove from cooking water and drain on a paper towel. Retain cooking water, keeping it at a low simmer.

In a large sauté pan add the butter and asparagus. Sauté. Season to taste with salt and pepper, and remove heat. Keep warm.

Poach the eggs. Follow instructions on page 115.

Divide asparagus onto four plates. With a slotted spoon remove eggs one at a time and pat on a paper towel to drain. Keeping the egg on your spoon, salt and pepper and place one egg on top of each plate of asparagus.

Dribble truffle oil over each dish and garnish with the Parmesan. Serve with a slice of good crusty bread.

Curry Quinoa

KRISTINA KELLOGG, ELM STREET BAKERY

SERVES 8

2 cups dry red quinoa,
  cooked

2 cups cilantro leaves

3 red bell peppers, roasted
  and diced

4 cups raw spinach

1/2 cup clover honey

1/4 cup curry powder

1 cup golden raisins

1 bunch scallions,
  chopped

1 cup sliced almonds,
  toasted

1/2 cup julienned carrots

1/4 cup olive oil

5 tablespoons apple cider
  vinegar

Salt and pepper, to taste

1/2 cup toasted coconut

Combine all ingredients except coconut in a large bowl. Season with salt and pepper and garnish with toasted coconut.

Greek Lamb Sliders

MARY ANN GIORDANO, GIGI'S CUCINA POVERA

SERVES 4

BURGERS

    2 pounds ground lamb
    3/4 onion, diced
    1/2 jalapeño, diced
    1 cup feta, crumbled
    1 egg
    1/4 cup fresh mint, chopped
    Salt and pepper, to taste
    12 slider buns

Place all ingredients in a mixing bowl. Using hands, combine thoroughly. Form meat into 12 slider-sized patties. Cook on hot grill, flipping patties until center reaches desired temperature.

TZATZIKI

    1/2 cucumber, seeded and shredded
    2 tablespoons fresh mint, chopped
    1 pint lebanah yogurt
    2 cloves garlic, minced
    2 tablespoons olive oil
    1 tablespoon red wine vinegar
    Salt and pepper, to taste

Combine all ingredients. Refrigerate until ready to use.

MANGO SALSA

    2 ripe mangos, peeled and diced
    1 red bell pepper, seeded and diced
    1/2 red onion, diced
    2 tablespoons fresh ginger, minced
    1/4 cup cilantro, stems removed and chopped
    Juice of 1 lime
    2 tablespoons olive oil
    Salt and pepper

Combine all ingredients. Refrigerate until ready to use.

Using 4 plates, divide buns, 3 to a plate. Place burger on bottom bun, top with tzatziki, salsa, and top bun.

Sesame Noodle Salad

MIKE ANDRZEJEWSKI, SEABAR

SERVES 4

SOY SESAME DRESSING

    1 cup soy sauce
    1/4 cup rice vinegar
    1/4 cup granulated sugar
    1/2 cup barbecue sauce
    1 tablespoon Sriracha Hot Chili Sauce
    1 tablespoon fresh ginger, grated
    1/3 cup sesame oil

Add all ingredients to a mixing bowl. Whisk until thoroughly combined. Set aside.

SALAD

    8 ounces cooked pasta, preferably thin noodles
        made of rice or wheat
    1/4 cup red bell pepper, diced
    1/4 cup red onion, diced
    1/4 cup scallions, sliced
    1 tablespoon toasted sesame seeds
    1/4 cup fresh cilantro, stems removed

In a large mixing bowl combine noodles with peppers, onion, and scallions. Add dressing to taste and mix thoroughly. Sprinkle with sesame seeds and cilantro leaves before serving.

Mussels with Herb-Caper Vinaigrette

JUSTIN BRINK, TORO TAPAS BAR

SERVES 4

1/2 cup champagne vinegar

1 lemon, juiced

3/4 cup canola oil

1/4 cup extra virgin olive oil

2 tablespoons fresh tarragon, chopped

2 tablespoons chives, chopped

2 tablespoons fresh dill, chopped

1/4 cup shallot, minced

1/3 cup capers, roughly chopped

1 teaspoon salt

2 pounds mussels, cleaned and debearded

2 cups white wine

Make a vinaigrette by combining vinegar, lemon juice, oils, herbs, shallot, capers, and salt in a bowl. Whisk and set aside.

Place pot on stove over high heat. Add the mussels and wine. Cover the pot and steam the mussels until they open. Discard any unopened mussels. Divide into 4 bowls and spoon vinaigrette over the top.

Rock Bottom Mussels

ALEX RUZZINE, RUZZINE'S ROCK BOTTOM

SERVES 4

4 pounds mussels, cleaned and debearded

6 cups sherry wine

4 teaspoons garlic, chopped

4 teaspoons shallots, chopped

1/2 cup Pernod pastis liqueur

2 cups tomatoes, diced

2 cups scallions, chopped

4 tablespoons unsalted butter

In a large pot over medium-high heat, add mussels, wine, chopped garlic, and shallots. Bring to a boil, and reduce to a simmer. Cook until the mussels have opened. Add the Pernod, tomatoes, and scallions. Cook until the alcohol has burned off, approximately 2 minutes. Remove from heat and swirl in butter. Discard any unopened mussels. Divide into 4 servings and serve with crusty bread.

BRUCE WIESZALA, EXECUTIVE CHEF, TABREE

After training and working as an engineer, Wieszala decided the kitchen was the place for him, and he applied all of the meticulous aspects of his personality and background to earning his education and climbing the ranks of many critically acclaimed Atlanta restaurants. His return to WNY was fortuitous, as he arrived just in time to become one of those leading the movement toward using fresh, local ingredients. Today he makes everything from scratch in the kitchen of Amherst's Tabree.

Loin of Spring Lamb with Potato Gnocchi, Spring Vegetables, Lamb Jus, and Mint Pesto

BRUCE WIESZALA, TABREE

SERVES 4

POTATO GNOCCHI

- 1/2 cup kosher salt
- 4 Russet potatoes
- 1 large egg, plus 1 large egg yolk
- 1/2 cup Parmesan, grated
- 1/4 teaspoon nutmeg, grated
- 1/4 teaspoon ground black pepper
- 1/8 teaspoon salt
- 1 cup all-purpose flour, plus more for dusting board and dough

Preheat oven to 425 degrees.

Spread a layer of kosher salt on a baking sheet and arrange the potatoes on top. Bake until a bit overcooked, about 60 minutes. Let sit until just cool enough to handle, cut in half, and scoop out the flesh, discarding the skins. Pass the potatoes through a potato ricer or grate them on the large holes of a box grater. Make a mound of potatoes on a clean counter or large cutting board, leaving a well in the center. To the well, add egg and yolk, cheese, nutmeg, salt, and pepper. Using clean hands, thoroughly mix the potatoes and contents of the well together. Sprinkle 1/2 the flour over the potatoes and, using your knuckles, press it into the potatoes. Fold the mass over on itself and press down again. Sprinkle more flour over the mixture, little by little, folding and pressing the dough until it just holds together, trying not to knead it. Work any dough on your fingers back into the potatoes. If the mixture is too dry, add another egg yolk or a little water. The dough should give under slight pressure. It will feel firm, but yielding.

Keeping the work surface and dough lightly floured, cut dough into 4 pieces. Roll each piece into a rope about a half inch in diameter. Cut into 1/2-inch-long pieces. A dough cutter works perfectly, but a knife will do. Lightly flour the cut gnocchi. Cook as is, or form into the classic gnocchi shape with a gnocchi board, ridged butter paddle, or the tines of a large fork turned upside down.

Scatter the gnocchi on baking sheets lined with parchment paper or waxed paper. If cooking the gnocchi the next day, freeze them. Alternatively, poach them now, drain and toss with a little olive oil, let cool, then refrigerate for several hours or overnight.

When ready to cook, bring a large pot of water to a high simmer (do not boil) and add salt. Drop gnocchi in, cooking for about 60 seconds after they rise to the surface. Remove gently, shake off excess water, toss with a little olive oil on a baking sheet, and set aside. Final cooking steps follow near the end of this recipe.

MINT PESTO

- 1/4 cup unsalted pistachios, shelled
- 3/4 cup mint leaves, stems removed
- 1/4 cup flat-leaf parsley, stems removed
- 2 scallions, cut into 4-inch pieces
- 2 medium garlic cloves, peeled
- 1/2 teaspoon lemon zest
- 2 tablespoons extra virgin olive oil
- Kosher salt, to taste

Pulse the pistachio nuts in a food processor once or twice until broken up into smaller pieces. Add the mint leaves, parsley, scallions, garlic, and lemon zest, and pulse again until chopped. With the machine on, add the olive oil in a thin stream and process until smooth. Season with salt. Cover and hold in refrigerator.

Tabree's Loin of Spring Lamb with Potato Gnocchi, Spring Vegetables, Lamb Jus, and Mint Pesto

LAMB JUS

Reserved lamb rib bones
1 shallot, thinly sliced
2 cloves garlic, peeled
1 sprig fresh thyme
2 bay leaves
2 cups chicken stock or low sodium chicken broth
1 cup dry red wine
Kosher salt
Freshly ground black pepper
1/2 teaspoon sherry vinegar (optional)

Preheat oven to 400 degrees. Place the rib bones on a baking sheet and roast for 20 minutes. Once roasted, place the bones in a heavy-bottomed sauce pot over high heat. Add shallot, garlic, thyme, bay leaves, chicken stock, and wine. Once it comes to a boil, reduce heat to low and simmer for 20 minutes. Remove from heat and strain sauce through a fine-mesh strainer into a container. Rinse the pot clean and return sauce to the pot. Place over medium-high heat and reduce by half. Remove from heat, add vinegar, season with salt and pepper to taste, cover, and keep warm.

VEGETABLES

3 dozen fava beans, double shucked
8 stalks fresh asparagus
Kosher salt

Have ready a large bowl of ice water, a slotted spoon, and a plate lined with a paper towel. Bring a large pot of water to boil over high heat. Meanwhile, prepare the asparagus, removing woody ends, place flat on a cutting board. Hold down the asparagus on the flowering end and, with a vegetable peeler, shave the stem into thin ribbons. Cut the flower ends in half lengthwise, set asparagus aside.
Before blanching the vegetables, add a couple tablespoons of salt to the boiling water. Drop the asparagus tips and fava beans into water for 30 seconds. Remove with the slotted spoon and plunge into bowl of ice water. After 2 minutes, remove the vegetables with a slotted spoon and place on a paper towel to dry.

SPRING LAMB

- 4 1/2 racks spring lamb*
- 4 tablespoons vegetable oil
- 4 tablespoons unsalted butter
- 4 sprigs fresh thyme, stems removed
- 2 cloves garlic, peeled
- Kosher salt
- Freshly ground pepper
- Fleur de sel, to taste

*Lamb racks can have rib bones removed except for one at the end of the loin for presentation. Or you can remove all the bones, if you prefer. Ask your butcher to assist you with this, but remember to reserve the bones for the jus.

Allow lamb to come to room temperature. Season with salt and pepper.

Preheat oven to 425 degrees. Place a large, heavy-bottomed sauté pan over medium-high heat. Add vegetable oil. Once the oil just begins to smoke, add butter. Once the butter begins to foam and turn golden brown, add the lamb loins, thyme, and garlic. If your pan isn't large enough for all of the racks, cook only 2 loins at a time. Allow the loins to develop a nice brown crust on one side, then turn over and brown the other side. Lay the seared loins on a baking sheet and roast in the oven for 7 minutes to reach medium-rare doneness. Remove the loins from the oven and place on a large plate lined with a paper towel. Cover with foil to rest. Discard garlic and thyme. While the lamb is resting, prepare the gnocchi.

PREPARE

- 2 tablespoons vegetable oil
- 1 tablespoon unsalted butter
- 1 tablespoon shallot, minced
- 1/2 cup dry white wine
- Spring vegetables (on page 57)
- Kosher salt
- Freshly ground black pepper
- 2 tablespoons flat-leaf parsley, chopped
- 1 tablespoon mint, chopped
- 1 tablespoon fleur de sel

Place a large sauté pan over medium-high heat. Add the oil. Once the oil begins to smoke, add

butter. Once the butter begins to foam and turn golden brown, add the gnocchi. When the gnocchi begins to brown on the bottom, add the shallot and toss. When the gnocchi browns on the reverse side, deglaze the pan with white wine. Add the asparagus, fava beans, salt, pepper, parsley, and mint. Toss together thoroughly and remove from heat.

PLATING

Divide the gnocchi and vegetables among four plates. Slice each lamb loin into 3 to 4 pieces and place over the gnocchi. Place a dollop of mint pesto on each plate and drizzle with the lamb jus. Finish with a sprinkle of fleur de sel over each lamb chop.

Emporer's Delight

ZHEN QIU (SAM) LAM, MING CAFE
4 SERVINGS

STIR FRY

- 1/3 pound prosciutto, diced
- 1/4 cup honey
- 5 tablespoons vegetable oil
- 8 baby bok choy
- 3 fresh oyster mushrooms, quartered
- 12 prawns
- 2 eggs, beaten
- 1/2 cup all-purpose flour
- 1/8 teaspoon salt
- 1 1/8 teaspoon white pepper
- 1 mango, peeled and diced
- 2 tablespoons ginger root, finely diced
- 4 garlic cloves, pressed
- 2 tablespoons scallion, chopped
- 1/2 red bell pepper, chopped
- 2 tablespoons fresh ginger, chopped
- 2 tablespoons hoisin sauce
- 1 tablespoon oyster sauce
- 2 tablespoons granulated sugar
- 1 1/2 tablespoons sherry wine

2 tablespoons soy sauce

1 tablespoon sesame oil

1/2 tablespoon white vinegar

1 teaspoon white pepper

1 tablespoon cornstarch

1 tablespoon bourbon

Place prosciutto in honey and cover. Marinate in the refrigerator overnight.

In a small pot of boiling water, add 1 tablespoon of the vegetable oil. Place bok choy into boiling water for 30 seconds. Remove using a slotted spoon, drain on a paper towel, and set aside. Repeat this method with the oyster mushroom. Deshell prawns and soak briefly in room-temperature water. Remove prawns and pat dry with a paper towel.

Prepare to batter prosciutto and prawns by setting up a small work area with two shallow bowls. In the first bowl, place the eggs. In the second bowl, combine the flour, salt, and white pepper. Individually coat the prawns in egg, allowing the excess to drain off. Move prawns to the second bowl, thoroughly dusting them in flour. Set aside on a plate.

Bring a wok to high heat. Add 2 tablespoons of the vegetable oil. Fry prawns for less than 1 minute. Drain on paper towels and set aside. Add the prosciutto and cook for approximately 30 seconds. Drain on paper towels and set aside. Follow the same steps with the mango, mushrooms, and bok choy, draining each of the fried ingredients on a paper towel. With all major ingredients set aside, begin the sauce by adding the ginger root, garlic, scallion, hoisin, oyster sauce, sugar, wine, soy sauce, sesame oil, and vinegar to the hot wok. Once combined, add 1 teaspoon of white pepper, cornstarch, and bourbon. Return the prawns, prosciutto, mushrooms, and mango to the sauce. Turn heat to low and allow ingredients to simmer for 30 to 45 seconds.

OSMANTHUS SAUCE

1 tablespoon vegetable oil

1 tablespoon fresh ginger, finely chopped

1 tablespoon brown sugar

1 tablespoon sherry wine

1 tablespoon cornstarch

1 1/2 tablespoons sweet osmanthus paste (available at Chinese markets)

In small sauce pan combine all ingredients, bring to a boil, and remove from heat. Dribble over stir fry for additional seasoning and serve immediately.

Ziti and Broccoli

CHEF MICHAEL CAPIZZI, MICHAEL'S ITALIAN RESTAURANT

SERVES 4

1 pound ziti

1 tablespoon salt

1 teaspoon garlic salt

1/2 teaspoon ground black pepper

2 teaspoons oregano, dry

3 teaspoons Pecorino Romano, grated

1 clove garlic, minced

1 1/2 cups extra virgin olive oil

2 heads broccoli, cleaned and cut into 1-inch florets

Bring 2 medium pots of water to a boil.
Prepare pasta in 1 pot, following the package directions.

In a small mixing bowl, whisk together garlic salt, pepper, oregano, cheese, garlic, and olive oil. Set aside.

In the second pot, add salt to water. Add broccoli and cook to desired doneness. Drain. In a large serving dish combine broccoli, pasta, and olive oil sauce. Serve alone or with grilled chicken or steak.

Duck with Thai Kale Salad

RICHARD BENZ, DICK AND JENNY'S

SERVES 8

DUCK

1 Long Island duck

1/4 cup kosher salt

1 teaspoon Chinese five
spice powder

1 teaspoon cracked black
pepper

4 cups canola oil

Butcher duck into quarters, creating 2 breasts and 2 leg-and-thigh quarters. Leaving skin and fat on the breasts and leg-and-thigh quarters, remove all excess exterior skin and fat from carcass and reserve. Combine salt, five spice powder, and pepper, and season breasts and thighs. Rest covered, in the refrigerator, overnight. Meanwhile, heat a heavy skillet. Combine reserved duck fat and skin with the oil and render until the fat liquefies and the skin becomes crispy. Let cool and strain, reserving the fat, and discarding the crispy skin. Keep fat in covered container in refrigerator until ready to use. The next day, prepare to confit duck, preheating oven to 325 degrees. Remove duck from refrigerator and place in an oven-proof casserole dish. Place duck fat in a sauce pan and return to liquid stage over medium heat. Pour over duck and bake in oven for 4 hours. Remove from oven and cool. The duck can be stored in its own fat in the refrigerator for up to 2 weeks. Forty-five minutes before serving, prepare salad (recipe on page 62) and allow to sit for up to 30 minutes at room temperature in order to reach peak flavor.

SALAD DRESSING

1/4 cup rice wine vinegar

1/3 cup honey

1/3 cup fish sauce

1/3 cup sesame oil

1/3 cup vegetable oil

1 tablespoon Dijon
mustard

1/4 teaspoon ground
cayenne pepper

In a bowl, combine all ingredients. Whisk until emulsified.

SALAD

- 1 bunch kale, washed, dried, cut into fine strips
- 1 bunch radish, washed, dried, cut into strips
- 3 carrots, peeled and julienned
- Half a fresh pineapple, peeled, cored, and cut into strips
- 1 tablespoon sesame seeds, toasted

Combine salad ingredients with dressing, toss well. Set aside.

ASSEMBLE

- Reserved duck fat
- Duck confit
- 1/3 cup hoisin sauce (garnish)

Remove duck confit pieces from oil. Cut both breasts in half and split drumsticks from thighs, creating 8 total pieces of duck. In a large heavy sauce pan, bring duck fat to 375 degrees. Fry duck, skin-side down, until skin is crispy. Turn each piece over once and cook another minute. Turn off pan, remove duck, and drain on a paper towel.

PLATING

Divide salad onto 8 plates. Place duck portion neatly on each. Garnish by dribbling small pools of hoisin sauce on plate.

Scallops Balboa

KRISTA VAN WAGNER, CURLY'S GRILL AND BANQUET CENTER

SERVES 4

- 1/4 cup unsalted butter, melted
- 2 pounds fresh sea scallops (U10 size recommended)
- 4 tablespoons shallots, minced
- 1/8 cup lemon juice
- 1/2 cup mushrooms
- 4 tablespoons fresh basil, chopped

- 1/2 cup dry white wine
- 1 cup heavy cream
- 8 artichoke hearts (canned and packed in oil), quartered

Melt half the butter in a sauté pan over medium high heat. Sear scallops on each side until golden brown, approximately 2 minutes per side. Remove from pan and keep warm.
Bring pan to medium-high heat. Add remaining butter and shallots. Allow shallots to become translucent, about 1 minute, and add lemon juice, mushrooms, and artichokes. Sauté until mushrooms are softened. Deglaze pan with the wine and keep on heat, reducing liquid by half. Add cream and bring to temperature. Add fresh basil leaves and toss. To serve, divide mushroom mixture between 4 plates. Add scallops to the top. Serve with large salad or steamed vegetables.

Vanilla Shortbread Domes

LUCI LEVERE, ELM STREET BAKERY

YIELDS 2 DOZEN COOKIES

- 1 1/2 cup all-purpose flour
- 1/2 cup, plus 1 tablespoon confectioner's sugar
- 1/4 cup cornstarch
- 1/4 teaspoon salt
- 1 cup cold unsalted butter, cubed
- 1 vanilla bean, split
- 1 1/2 teaspoons vanilla extract
- Granulated sugar for rolling

Preheat oven to 325 degrees. In a food processor, place flour, sugar, cornstarch, and salt. Pulse to combine. Add butter, contents of scraped vanilla bean, and vanilla extract. Pulse until a smooth dough forms. Form cookies by scooping dough with a small ice cream scoop. Bake on a cookie sheet until edges are golden brown. Let cool and roll in granulated sugar.

Ta Kwai Yai (Burmese Black Rice Pudding)

KEVIN LIN, SUN RESTAURANT

SERVES 10

1 1/4 cups black rice

2 cups water

1 can coconut milk (13.5 ounces)

3/4 cup granulated sugar

1 sweet potato, peeled and sliced

1 banana, peeled and sliced

1/8 teaspoon salt

Place black rice and 1 cup of the water in a rice cooker, or cook on the stovetop following package instructions. Cool.

In a medium-sized sauce pan, heat coconut milk and remaining water. Stir and bring to medium heat. Add sugar and stir until dissolved. Add sweet potato. Cook for another 10 to 15 minutes. Place rice in a large mixing bowl. Add milk and sweet potato mixture until pudding has reached desired consistency. Fold in sliced bananas and serve.

SUMMER

Gazpacho Cocktail

JON KAREL, VERA PIZZERIA

YIELDS 1 DRINK

2 ounces New Amsterdam Gin

1 ounce St. Germain

3/4 ounce fresh lemon juice

1 barspoon Sriracha Hot Chili Sauce

2 cucumber slices

Ice

Bruise cucumber slices. Add all ingredients to a cocktail shaker, reserving some ice for glass. Shake vigorously. Strain over ice.

Chicken Satay with Peanut Sauce

JOE GEORGE, 20TH CENTURY CLUB

YIELDS 32 PIECES

SKEWERS

2 pounds boneless chicken, beef, or lamb

1/4 cup vegetable oil

2 tablespoons fresh lemongrass, chopped

2 cloves garlic, chopped

2 teaspoons Thai curry paste

2 tablespoons honey

1 tablespoon nam pla (Thai fish sauce)

Bamboo skewers

Peanut sauce (see recipe)

Cut the meat into thin strips about 4 inches long. Lightly pound the strips of meat with a mallet, or with the back of a small skillet. Thread the strips onto 6-inch bamboo skewers that have been soaked briefly in water. Make the marinade by combining in a blender the vegetable oil, lemongrass, garlic, curry paste, honey, and fish sauce, processing until smooth. Brush the skewered meat with the marinade and allow it to marinate covered in the refrigerator for 1 hour. Cook the satay in an oven or on a grill for a couple minutes, or until the meat is just done (care should be taken to thoroughly cook chicken). Serve while hot with peanut sauce.

PEANUT SAUCE

2 tablespoons vegetable oil

1/2 small onion, diced

2 cloves garlic, minced

1 teaspoon Thai curry paste

2 tablespoons granulated sugar

1 cup coconut milk

1 ounce lime juice

4 ounces rice wine vinegar

1 1/2 cups low sodium chicken broth

1 1/2 cups creamy peanut butter

Heat the oil in a small saucepan, add the onion and garlic, and sauté for a minute or two. Add the curry paste and the sugar and sauté another minute. Stir in the milk, juice, vinegar, and broth. Bring the liquid to a simmer and cook for about 10 minutes. Stir in the peanut butter and cook another 5 minutes. Transfer the sauce to a blender and process until smooth. Serve warm.

Corn Fritters with Chili Lime Aioli

MARY ANN GIORDANO, GIGI'S CUCINA POVERA

SERVES 4

FRITTERS:

4 ears corn on the cob

2 teaspoons ground cumin

1 teaspoon garlic, chopped

1/4 cup olive oil

2 red peppers, diced

- 1/2 red onion, diced
- 1 cup fresh cilantro, chopped
- 3 eggs
- 1 cup milk
- 2 cups all-purpose flour
- 1 cup cornmeal
- 1/2 cup granulated sugar
- Salt and pepper, to taste
- Oil for frying

Preheat oven to 350 degrees. Remove corn kernels from cobs; discard cobs. In a mixing bowl, combine corn, cumin, garlic, and olive oil. Spread mixture onto a sheet tray and cover with foil. Bake for 30 minutes. Remove from oven and cool to room temperature. Combine corn mixture with peppers, onion, cilantro, eggs, milk, flour, cornmeal, sugar, salt, and pepper. Mix thoroughly. On the stovetop, in a heavy-bottomed pan, heat approximately 3 inches of cooking oil to 325 degrees. Drop rounded spoonfuls of corn batter into oil, and cook, until fritters turn golden brown. Remove from oil using a slotted spoon and drain on paper towels.

CHILI LIME AIOLI:

- 1 1/2 cups mayonnaise
- 3 tablespoons Sriracha Hot Chili Sauce
- 1 tablespoon ancho chili powder
- 2 tablespoons lime juice
- Salt and pepper, to taste

Mix all ingredients in a medium-size mixing bowl. Blend well and serve with warm corn fritters.

Marinated Shrimp, Tomato, and Mozzarella Salad

JOE GEORGE, 20TH CENTURY CLUB

SERVES 4

- 2/3 cup olive oil
- 1/3 cup white wine vinegar
- 1 clove garlic, minced
- 4 fresh basil leaves, chopped
- 1/4 teaspoon salt
- 1/4 teaspoon ground black pepper
- 9 gulf shrimp, peeled and deveined
- 2 medium tomatoes
- 4 ounces fresh Mozzarella, sliced

In a small bowl combine the oil, vinegar, garlic, basil, salt, and pepper; whisk together and set aside. Poach the shrimp in simmering, lightly salted water for about 4 minutes. Drain the shrimp and transfer them to a small bowl. Pour half the vinaigrette over the shrimp and refrigerate for 1 hour. Slice the tomatoes and arrange them on chilled plates, alternate the slices of tomatoes with slices of Mozzarella. Drain the shrimp and arrange them on top of the tomatoes and cheese. Dribble vinaigrette over the salads.

Lyonnaise Salad

EDWARD FORSTER, THE WORKSHOP

Forster, a Buffalo native, returned to the region after completing his education at Culinary Institute of America and working in some of Chicago's finest restaurants, including Graham Elliott and Blackbird. His firm grasp of modernist cooking techniques earned him early praise and excellent reviews as the opening executive chef at Mike A @Hotel Lafayette. He is currently developing his next project, The Workshop.

Lyonnaise Salad

EDWARD FORSTER, THE WORKSHOP

SERVES 8

POTATO AND BACON TERRINE

- 3-inch slab of bacon, sliced thin
- 6 Idaho potatoes, peeled, reserved in cold water
- 1/2 cup unsalted butter, clarified
- Salt to taste
- 3 tablespoons thyme leaves, stems removed

Preheat oven to 350 degrees. Place bacon flat on a parchment-lined baking sheet. Bake until partially cooked, approximately 8 minutes. Remove from oven, carefully draining bacon fat. Reserve fat for dressing recipe.

Pat potatoes dry and slice 1/8-inch thick. Add clarified butter to a large, nonstick sauté pan. Heat over medium heat until warm. Add potato slices. Season with salt and thyme leaves. Remove from heat. Set potatoes aside to cool. In a plastic-lined terrine mold, place a single layer of potatoes on the bottom, overlapping the potatoes by 1/3-inch, until the bottom of the pan is completely covered. Lay bacon slices over potatoes, again slightly overlapping. Repeat alternating layers of potato and bacon until terrine is filled slightly above the rim, pressing gently to ensure a well-packed terrine. Cover with parchment paper and aluminum foil, and bake terrine mold in a water bath until internal temperature reads 180 degrees on a probe thermometer. Once cooked, remove the terrine from the bath. Set a weight atop and press overnight, in the refrigerator, until chilled through. Cut into 1/3-inch slices and sear on each side to serve.

SHERRY DRESSING

- 2 shallots, peeled
- 3 sprigs thyme, stems removed
- 2 tablespoons Dijon mustard
- 2 egg yolks
- 1 cup sherry vinegar
- 2 tablespoons bacon fat
- 1 quart canola oil
- Salt and pepper to taste

Purée shallot, thyme, Dijon, and yolks with vinegar in a high-speed blender. Add bacon fat and oil, emulsifying the fats. Add ice water to thin, if necessary. Season with salt and pepper to taste. Set aside.

SALAD ASSEMBLY

- 4 heads frisée lettuce
- 8 eggs, poached
- 4 chives, cut into 1-inch pieces

Poach eggs. See page 115 for instructions. Cut frisée heads in half. Remove and discard the dark green exterior leaves. Wash, spin, and dry on a paper towel-lined tray. Season frisée with dressing, salt, pepper, and chives.

Arrange half a head of frisée, a slice of warm terrine, chives, and an egg on each plate. Lightly dress plate with small amounts of remaining dressing.

Egg Quesadilla with Roasted Tomato Salsa

RICH HOLLISTER, CANTINA LOCO

SERVES 2

SALSA

- 4 large tomatoes, cored and scored with an "x" on bottom
- 1/2 medium Spanish onion, peeled and chopped

into several large pieces
- 1 clove garlic
- 1 fresh jalapeño, cleaned
- 1/4 cup vegetable oil
- Salt, to taste
- Juice of half a lime
- 1/2 bunch cilantro, stems removed

Preheat oven to 450 degrees. Coat tomatoes, onion, garlic, and jalapeño with oil. Arrange on a foil-lined baking sheet and place in oven. Roast until tomatoes begin to char and the skin at the "x" begins to pull away from the tomato. Remove from oven and allow ingredients to cool to the touch. Peel skin from tomatoes. Place all roasted ingredients into food processor and pulse a few times. Add salt, lime, and cilantro, and pulse again. Set salsa aside. Will keep in a refrigerator for 3 to 4 days.

QUESADILLA

- 4 large eggs
- 4 8-inch flour tortillas
- 1/8 cup vegetable oil
- 1/2 cup cooked bacon, crumbled
- 1/2 cup fresh or canned green chiles, diced
- 1 cup shredded cheese (Cheddar, Monterey Jack, or Colby)
- 1 ripe avocado, peeled and sliced
- 1/2 cup sour cream
- 8 jalapeño slices (fresh or jarred)
- 8 fresh cilantro leaves, stems removed

Beat and scramble the eggs. Hold aside. In large nonstick skillet, heat a small amount of the oil. Place first tortilla in and spin to distribute the oil. Atop the tortilla, evenly spread just under half the cheese, half the bacon, eggs, and the chiles. Sprinkle a little cheese over the top (this will help the quesadilla stay together). Top with a second tortilla and drizzle a little oil over the top. When the bottom tortilla browns, turn over, spinning slightly to disperse oil. Once browned, remove and repeat the process.

To serve, cut each quesadilla into 4 wedges. Top with avocado, a dollop of sour cream, jalapeño slices, and cilantro leaves. Spoon salsa onto each plate and serve.

Panzanella Salad

MARK SCIORTINO, MARCO'S ITALIAN RESTAURANT

SERVES 4

VINAIGRETTE

1 1/2 cup olive oil

1 cup red wine vinegar

Salt and pepper, to taste

1 teaspoon garlic, minced

1 teaspoon pesto

In a small mixing bowl combine oil, vinegar, salt, pepper, garlic, and pesto. Whisk together and set aside.

SALAD

2 loaves stale Italian bread or baguette, cubed

1 cup low-moisture Mozzarella, grated

1/2 cup pepperoni, sliced

1/4 cup sweet onion, diced

1/4 cup hot Hungarian pepper, diced

1/4 cup carrot, shredded

1/4 cup celery, diced

1/4 cup red pepper, diced

1/4 cup canned artichoke hearts, halved

10 cherry tomatoes, halved

1/4 cup green olives, sliced

In a large bowl combine bread, Mozzarella, pepperoni, onion, hot pepper, carrot, celery, red pepper, artichokes, tomatoes, and olives. Mix gently and thoroughly. Add the vinaigrette and toss until bread cubes are well coated.

Chilled Pea Purée with Fresh Basil

KEITH DULAK, TRATTORIA AROMA

SERVES 4

4 cups homemade chicken stock

1 tablespoon kosher salt

2 cups fresh snow peas, chopped

2 cups fresh peas, shucked

1/2 teaspoon black pepper

1 tablespoon fresh basil, chiffonade

In a pot over high heat bring stock to a rolling boil. Add salt. Remove from the heat and add the snow peas and fresh peas. Let stand for 5 minutes. Purée stock and peas using a stick blender or a countertop blender on high. Strain through a fine mesh strainer into a container resting on ice. Season with salt and pepper. Allow to cool in the refrigerator. Serve in individual bowls topped with fresh basil.

Black Linguine with Calamari, Zucchini, Peperoncino, and Bottarga

MICHAEL OBARKA, RISTORANTE LOMBARDO

SERVES 4

BLACK LINGUINE

2 cups all-purpose flour, plus a little more, if needed

1 tablespoon extra virgin olive oil

1 tablespoon squid ink

Salt

2 eggs, lightly beaten

Combine flour, oil, ink, and salt into the bowl of a stand mixer fitted with a dough hook. Slowly add the eggs, mixing on low until the mass becomes a ball of dough. Let the machine knead on medium speed for at least 10 minutes. Remove dough from the mixing bowl and allow to rest, covered, for 30 minutes.

Cut the ball into four equal parts. One quarter at a time, knead the dough into a rectangular shape. If using a pasta rolling machine, start at the widest setting. Adjust the opening to a smaller setting every time, until you roll through the second smallest setting. Otherwise, roll dough out on well-floured board until pasta is 1/16-inch thick. Dust pasta sheet with flour and repeat with the other three wedges of dough.

Cut each sheet into linguine-width noodles. Dust with flour and spread on a cookie sheet or counter to keep from sticking together.

GARLIC BREADCRUMBS

- 1 cup panko breadcrumbs
- 2 tablespoons olive oil
- Salt and pepper, to taste
- 3 cloves garlic, finely minced

Preheat oven to 400 degrees. Combine all ingredients in a mixing bowl. Spread evenly on a baking sheet and place in oven. Check crumbs, stirring gently, every few minutes until evenly golden brown and fragrant. Transfer to a plate and cool.

CALAMARI

- 1/4 cup extra virgin olive oil
- 1 zucchini, julienned
- 1 small onion, diced
- 4 cloves garlic, minced
- 1 pound calamari tubes and tentacles, tubes cut into 1/4-inch rings
- 1/4 cup lemon juice
- 1 batch Black Linguine
- Salt and pepper, to taste
- Peperoncino (red pepper flakes), to taste
- 1/2 cup fresh basil leaves, torn
- 1/4 cup Garlic Breadcrumbs
- 1 lemon, zested
- Bottarga, grated to taste (optional)

Put a large pot of salted water on to boil. Warm olive oil in a large skillet over medium-high heat. Add zucchini, onion, and garlic. Sweat until just softened. Add the calamari and cook lightly. Add the lemon juice. Remove from heat temporarily.

Drop the linguine into the boiling water and cook about 2 minutes, or until floating and tender. Drain and add the pasta to the skillet. Return the skillet to medium heat, season with salt, pepper, and chili flakes.

Add the torn basil, toss thoroughly, and divide among four pasta bowls. Top with breadcrumbs, a small amount of grated bottarga, if using, and lemon zest.

Chicken Savannah

KEVIN ALLEN, ADAM'S RIB

SERVES 4

- 4 boneless skinless chicken breasts
- 1/2 cup all-purpose flour
- 1/2 teaspoon salt
- 1/8 teaspoon white pepper
- 3 tablespoons vegetable oil
- 2 ounces Southern Comfort
- 1 14-ounce can sliced peaches, in syrup
- 1/2 cup heavy cream
- 1/2 cup pecans, chopped
- 3 scallions, sliced

Preheat oven to 400 degrees. Pat chicken dry. Combine flour, salt, and pepper in a shallow bowl. Dredge chicken in seasoned flour, coating thoroughly.

Heat vegetable oil in a large skillet over medium heat. Add chicken, cooking on both sides until internal temperature of 160 degrees has been reached and outside is golden brown. Drain oil from pan. Remove pan from heat and add Southern Comfort. Return to heat. Add the canned peaches and 1/4 cup of the syrup. Add cream and pecans. Transfer chicken, peaches, pecans, and sauce to an ovenproof dish. Place in oven, cooking for 10 minutes. Remove from oven and plate, garnishing each dish with scallions.

KEVIN RICHERT, CO-OWNER/EXECUTIVE CHEF, SMOKE ON THE WATER
CO-OWNER, TORCHES; THE GARAGE DELI

Richert, along with his wife, Lindsay; brother, JJ; and sister-in-law, Cynthia, own and operate some of the area's most quirky and fun restaurants. With a passion for motorcycles, tattoos, and great food, the Richert brothers and their wives have introduced bold flavors and big personalities to Buffalo's growing restaurant scene.

Pork Belly Tacos recipe on following page.

Pork Belly Tacos

KEVIN RICHERT, SMOKE ON THE WATER

SERVES 8

PORK

1 fresh pork belly

1/2 cup dry barbecue rub

1 liter ginger ale

2 cups maraschino
cherries and juice

4 cloves garlic, peeled

1 red onion, chopped

1/2 cup sweet chili sauce

24 taco shells

Sour cream (optional)

Hot sauce (optional)

Preheat oven to 350 degrees. Rub the pork belly with the dry barbecue rub and grill or sear in hot pan until exterior is charred. In a deep roasting pan add ginger ale, cherries with cherry juice, garlic, and onion. Place belly in pan and cover with foil. Cook in the oven for 3-1/2 to 4 hours. When done, a knife inserted into the meat should turn with little resistance. Remove pan from oven. Uncover and remove belly to rest. Cool slightly and slice. Place meat in taco shells and garnish with slaw (recipe follows). Garnish with additional sour cream or hot sauce.

SLAW

1 red onion, grated

1 cucumber, seeded and
grated

1 carrot, grated

2 tablespoons granulated
sugar

1 small bunch radishes,
thinly sliced

3 tablespoons rice wine
vinegar

1 cup iceberg lettuce,
shredded

Juice of 1 lime

4 tablespoons pickled
ginger

4 tablespoons sour cream

Gently toss all ingredients together in a large mixing bowl. Dress each taco with slaw.

Loco Chicken Tomatillo

RICH HOLLISTER, CANTINA LOCO

SERVES 4

SAUCE

- 2 cloves garlic, minced
- 1 medium onion, chopped
- 1 poblano pepper, seeded and chopped
- 1 jalapeño pepper, seeded and chopped
- 2 pounds tomatillos, husk removed, cored, and coarse chopped
- 2 cups low-sodium chicken broth
- 2 teaspoons salt
- 2 teaspoons ground cumin
- 2 tablespoons granulated sugar
- 1 tablespoon rice wine vinegar
- 1/2 bunch cilantro, chopped

In a medium sauce pan, sauté garlic, onion, and peppers until soft. Add tomatillos, broth, salt, cumin, sugar, and vinegar. Simmer 20 minutes. Transfer to a food processor and add cilantro. Purée and set aside.

CHICKEN

- 1 cup all-purpose flour
- 2 teaspoons ground cumin
- 1 teaspoon ground coriander
- 1 teaspoon chile powder
- 4 large boneless, skinless chicken thighs
- 3 tablespoons vegetable oil
- 1/2 cup Pepper Jack, shredded
- 1/2 cup Cheddar, shredded
- Cilantro leaves for garnish

Preheat oven to 425 degrees. Combine flour, cumin, coriander, and chile powder in a shallow dish. Dredge chicken thighs, shaking off any excess flour. Heat oil in a large skillet. Sear chicken breasts, approximately 2 minutes on each side. Transfer chicken to an ovenproof dish. Top with sauce and cheeses. Bake 20 minutes. Garnish with cilantro leaves.

Seafood Stew

JOE CHAMBERS,
RUSSELL'S STEAKS, CHOPS AND MORE

SERVES 4

- 4 4-ounce lobster tails
- 5 tablespoons olive oil
- 1 cup onion, diced
- 2 links Italian sausage, cut into thick slices
- 6 garlic cloves, sliced
- 2 tablespoons shallots, minced
- 1 1/2 cups white wine
- 1 1/2 cups fish stock
- Pinch of saffron threads
- 12 middleneck clams, cleaned
- 2 1/2 cups canned plum tomatoes
- 8 large shrimp, deveined
- 4 large sea scallops
- Salt and pepper, to taste
- 8 slices ciabatta bread
- 1 tablespoon fresh basil, chopped
- 1 tablespoon flat-leaf parsley, chopped
- 1/8 cup Parmesan, grated

Crack the lobster tails and set aside. In a large, heavy-bottomed pot, heat 2 tablespoons of the olive oil. Add sausage slices and onions. Allow the sausage and onion to lightly brown. Add garlic and shallots. When the garlic begins to brown, add white wine, fish stock, and saffron. Bring to a boil. Add clams and tomatoes. Cover and cook for 2 to 3 minutes. Add shrimp, scallops, lobster tails, salt, and pepper. Lower heat to a simmer and allow the shrimp and lobster to cook through.

Meanwhile, heat a large skillet. Brush ciabatta with remaining oil, herbs, and Parmesan. Cook bread quickly on each side. Divide stew into 4 bowls and serve each dish with slices of crispy bread for dipping.

Cuban Burger

JAY MANNO, SOHO BURGER BAR

SERVES 8

JALAPEÑO MUSTARD

1 jalapeño, roasted

1 cup Dijon mustard

1/2 cup whole grain
   mustard

1 lime

1/4 cup honey

Salt and pepper, to taste

Add all ingredients to a food processor. Pulse until combined.

BURGER

4 pounds ground pork butt

1 tablespoon fennel seed

1 tablespoon red pepper
   flakes

1 tablespoon cumin

1 tablespoon salt

1/2 tablespoon black
   pepper

1/2 cup parsley, chopped

8 slices Swiss cheese

8 slices deli ham

Dill pickle chips

8 burger buns

Combine pork, fennel, red pepper, cumin, salt, pepper, and parsley in a large mixing bowl. Using hands, mix seasoning into the meat. Form eight 8-ounce burgers. Using a grill or cast-iron pan, cook burgers to desired doneness. Before removing from heat, melt a slice of Swiss on top of each patty. To serve, place patties on buns. Add a slice of ham and dill pickle chips to each. Spread jalapeño mustard generously on the top bun.

Pickle-Brined Boneless Fried Chicken

CHRISTOPHER SALVATI, JOE'S DELI

SERVES 4

CHICKEN

- 8 3–4 ounce boneless, skinless chicken breasts
- 4 cups dill pickle juice
- 5 cups all-purpose flour
- 1 tablespoon black pepper
- 2 tablespoons salt
- 1 tablespoon garlic powder
- 2 teaspoons cayenne pepper
- 4 cups buttermilk
- Vegetable oil or shortening for frying

Cover chicken with dill pickle juice and marinate in the refrigerator overnight. Remove from refrigerator and discard brine. Pat chicken dry. Combine flour with pepper, salt, garlic powder, and cayenne in a shallow dish. Set up a breading station by adding buttermilk to a second shallow dish. One piece at a time, dredge the chicken first in the flour mixture, shaking off any excess. Then dip it into the buttermilk and return to the seasoned flour, covering thoroughly and shaking off any excess. Set aside until all chicken has been battered.

On the stovetop, heat a half inch of oil or shortening in a cast-iron skillet. Fry chicken approximately 6 minutes on each side, until internal temperature reaches 160 degrees. Remove from pan and drain on a paper towel.

Note: A whole, bone-in chicken, cut into eight pieces, can also be used. Cooking time will be closer to 9 minutes per side in a cast-iron skillet.

HONEY MUSTARD

- 1 cup mustard
- 1/2 cup honey
- 1/2 cup mayonnaise

Combine all ingredients. Serve chicken on rolls or biscuits with a dollop of honey mustard.

Fried Chicken with Carrot Walnut Buttermilk Biscuits

JENNIFER BOYE,
MANSION ON DELAWARE AVENUE

SERVES 4

CHICKEN

1 quart buttermilk

1 cup sour cream

2 tablespoons kosher salt

1 tablespoon freshly ground black pepper

1/4 cup hot sauce

1 tablespoon garlic powder

1 tablespoon onion powder

1 small onion, thinly sliced

2 chicken drumsticks

2 chicken thighs

2 large chicken breasts, halved

2 cups all-purpose flour

2 teaspoons kosher salt

8 cups vegetable oil for frying

2 stalks celery

Combine buttermilk, sour cream, salt, pepper, hot sauce, garlic powder, onion powder, and onion slices in a bowl. Submerge chicken in the brine, cover, and refrigerate for at least 12 hours (and up to 24).

Add flour and kosher salt to a shallow dish. Remove chicken from brine and place directly into flour. Coat evenly.

In a heavy-bottomed pot, heat vegetable oil to 365 degrees. Add chicken and celery. Fry chicken, rotating occasionally, until internal temperature reaches 160 degrees. Chicken may need to be fried in batches to avoid overcrowding. If chicken is browning too quickly, reduce heat slightly. Chicken should take at least 12 minutes to cook completely. Discard celery. Drain on paper towels and serve immediately. Serve with Carrot and Walnut Biscuits.

CARROT WALNUT BUTTERMILK BISCUITS

3 cups all-purpose flour

1 teaspoon kosher salt

2 teaspoons baking powder

1/2 teaspoon baking soda

2 sticks unsalted butter, chilled and cut into small pieces

1/4 cup scallion, sliced

1 cup buttermilk, chilled

1/2 cup carrot juice, chilled

1/2 cup walnuts, chopped

Preheat oven to 350 degrees. In a large bowl, combine flour, salt, baking powder, and baking soda. Add butter and combine with your fingers until the butter is the size of small peas. Add the scallions and walnuts and mix until combined. Mix in buttermilk and carrot juice. Handle as little as possible, combining until a ball of dough has formed. The dough should be slightly sticky. Roll it out onto a well-floured surface, creating a 1/2-inch rectangle. Use a biscuit cutter or the mouth of a glass to cut rounds from the dough. Place biscuits on a lightly sprayed baking sheet and bake until the surface of each biscuit is golden brown and the middle is cooked through, 12 to 15 minutes. Serve warm with butter.

Berkshire Pork Chop with Mango BBQ Glaze

CHARLIE MALLIA, 800 MAPLE RESTAURANT

SERVES 6

MANGO BBQ GLAZE

2 tablespoons vegetable oil

1 teaspoon fresh ginger, minced

2 cloves garlic, minced

1 small onion, diced

1 16-ounce can mango nectar

2 cups ketchup

1/2 cup amber agave syrup

1 teaspoon liquid smoke

2 teaspoons ground coriander

2 teaspoons chipotle powder

1 teaspoon crushed red pepper

Salt and pepper, to taste

Over medium heat warm oil in a large sauce pan. Add ginger, garlic, and onion. Cook until translucent. Add mango nectar, ketchup, agave syrup, liquid smoke, and spices. Stirring frequently, simmer until liquid is reduced by one-third.

PORK CHOP

6 10-ounce Berkshire pork chops (all-natural thick cut pork chops may be substituted)

Salt and pepper, to taste

Season pork chops. Grill until they reach an internal temperature of 140 degrees, 8 to 10 minutes per side. Remove from grill and let rest. Serve with Mango BBQ Glaze.

JENNIFER K. MARABELLA, EXECUTIVE CHEF, SIENA
Marabella is a locally trained chef with a passion for classical and contemporary food preparation and techniques. As executive chef at Amherst's popular eatery, Siena, she is able to explore both traditional and innovative offerings, with a menu featuring old world wood-fired pizzas alongside new world takes on appetizers and entrees.
What is your favorite aspect of being a chef?
"The thrill is what I live for."

Bronzini with Mussels, Scallion, and Tomato from Siena.

Bronzini with Mussels, Scallion, and Tomato

JENNIFER K. MARABELLA, SIENA

SERVES 4

4 bronzino fillets, tails
attached

6 tablespoons olive oil

1 medium onion, diced

1 cup cherry tomatoes,
halved

16 mussels, debearded

1 cup dry white wine

1/2 cup seafood or fish
stock

1/8 teaspoon crushed red
pepper

Salt and pepper, to taste

2 bunches flat-leaf parsley,
chopped

2 bunches scallion greens,
sliced

2 tablespoons roasted
garlic

1/2 cup canned tomato
strips

1 tablespoon unsalted
butter

10 basil leaves, torn

4 lemon wedges

Season fish fillets with salt and pepper. On the stovetop, heat a heavy skillet over medium-high heat. Coat the pan with olive oil until it is almost smoking. Add fish to the pan, flesh side down. Cook 2 to 3 minutes until golden and cooked through. Remove fish from the pan and place flesh side up on a warm platter. Return pan to heat and add onion, cherry tomatoes, and mussels. Deglaze with white wine. Add stock and cook until liquid is reduced by half. Add crushed red pepper, salt and pepper, half the parsley, and scallions. Stir in roasted garlic and tomato strips.

Continue to cook and stir the pan until all the mussels open and sauce begins to develop.

Add butter and remaining parsley. Stir, until butter melts. Pour mussels and sauce over each fillet. Top with basil and serve with lemon wedges.

Crème Bulgare

PATRICK LANGO, WHITE COW DAIRY SHOP

YIELDS 1 QUART

1 quart heavy cream
2 tablespoons plain yogurt
1 vanilla bean, split
1/4 cup raw honey
3–4 drops rose water
1 teaspoon brandy (optional)

In a double boiler, heat the cream and vanilla bean to 190 degrees, stirring occasionally. Remove from the heat, and let sit, covered, for 15 to 20 minutes. Make an ice bath in a large bowl. Place the cream and the top portion of the double boiler in the bath, uncovered. Stir until the temperature is reduced to 120 degrees.

Remove the pan from the bath and add stir in the yogurt. Cover with a lid and wrap the pan with kitchen towels. Leave the cream in a warm spot, undisturbed, for 24 hours.

Once the appropriate amount of time has passed, unwrap the creme and remove the lid. Discard the vanilla bean and stir in the raw honey, rose water, and brandy, if desired.

Chill well. Serve with fresh fruit or as a topping for baked goods.

Creme Brulee French Toast with Almond Honey Mascarpone

CRAIG MOORE, BATAVIA DOWNS GRANDSTANDS BAR AND GRILL

SERVES 4

2 cups strawberries, cleaned and quartered
1/4 cup granulated sugar
2 cups Mascarpone
1/4 cup cream cheese, softened
2 tablespoons honey
1/4 cup sliced almonds, toasted
3/4 pound salted butter, softened
8 large eggs
1 vanilla bean or 2 teaspoons vanilla extract
1/4 cup heavy cream
1 stale French baguette
3/4 cup brown sugar
2 tablespoons confectioner's sugar

In a small bowl combine the strawberries and the granulated sugar. Mix gently and set aside.

In a medium-size mixing bowl, combine Mascarpone, cream cheese, honey, and all but 2 tablespoons of the toasted almonds. Mix thoroughly and set aside.

Preheat oven to 350 degrees. Grease a large baking sheet with the butter and set aside.

In a large bowl, beat together eggs, vanilla, and heavy cream. Cut the French bread into 1-inch pieces, discarding the ends. Soak the French bread slices in the egg mixture, allowing enough time for the bread to thoroughly soak the mixture up. Remove the bread from the mixture and allow the excess to drain off. Place the slices on the buttered sheet tray. Spread brown sugar evenly onto one side of each piece of bread. Bake in the oven, uncovered, for 15 to 20 minutes. Take care that the sugar doesn't burn; it should be melted and the bread browned along its edges. Remove from the oven and allow to the bread to cool slightly.

PREPARE

To plate, place a scoop of the Mascarpone mixture on a plate, and lean two pieces of French toast over the top. Dress the plate with strawberries and garnish with confectioner's sugar and the remaining toasted almonds.

FALL

Honey Badger Cocktail

TIM BROWN, THE EAGLE HOUSE RESTAURANT

YIELDS 1 DRINK

2 ounces honey syrup (recipe below)
1 1/2 ounces Citron Vodka
1 1/2 ounces Bombay Sapphire
1/2 ounce vanilla vodka
Splash of orange juice
Juice of 1 lemon
Lemon twist for garnish

For the honey syrup, heat equal parts honey and water in a sauce pan. Stir until fully incorporated. Chill before using.

To make the drink, add all ingredients to a cocktail shaker with ice. Strain into a martini glass.

Garnish with a lemon twist.

Rocket Wings

CHRIS DORSANEO, LLOYD TACO TRUCKS

SERVES 4

CUMIN LIME CREMA

1/2 cup sour cream
1/4 cup mayonnaise
1 teaspoon garlic powder
1/2 teaspoon ground cumin
1 teaspoon fresh lime juice
1/4 teaspoon salt
1 tablespoon Queso Fresco, crumbled

Combine all ingredients in a small mixing bowl. Store in refrigerator at least 20 minutes before serving, allowing flavors to come together.

PICKLED CARROT

2 large carrots, peeled and julienned
1/3 cup white vinegar
3 tablespoons granulated sugar
1 dried oregano

In a small saucepan, bring sugar, vinegar, and dried oregano to a boil, then chill in refrigerator. Once brine is chilled, toss with carrots and allow to sit for 20 minutes. Set aside.

WINGS

1 quart vegetable oil for frying
1 1/2 pounds chicken wings
1/4 cup Lloyd's Rocket Sauce
1/4 cup unsalted butter, melted
2 tablespoons fresh cilantro, chopped

Heat oil to 350 degrees in a Dutch oven or tabletop fryer. Slowly and carefully drop wings into oil to avoid spatter. Fry wings for 8 to 15 minutes, depending on desired crispiness. Using tongs, remove wings from oil and drain on paper towels. Melt butter in small saucepan. Add Rocket Sauce and mix.

Transfer wings to a large bowl and toss with butter mixture and half the fresh cilantro. To serve, place sauced wings on a platter with Pickled Carrots and Cumin Lime Crema. Garnish dish with remaining cilantro.

Stuffed Banana Peppers with Red Creole Sauce

ADAM ZIMPFER, FAT BOB'S SMOKEHOUSE

SERVES 6

RED CREOLE SAUCE

1 pound tomatoes, cored and quartered
3 cups onion, quartered

1/8 cup garlic cloves, smashed

1/2 tablespoon liquid smoke

1/2 tablespoon spice rub

1/2 teaspoon dry thyme

1/2 teaspoon dry oregano

1/2 teaspoon dry basil

1/2 teaspoon ground cumin

1/4 teaspoon cayenne

1/2 cup tomato juice

3/4 cup water

Salt and pepper, to taste

Preheat oven to 350 degrees. Combine tomatoes, onions, and garlic in a mixing bowl. Add liquid smoke, rub, thyme, oregano, basil, cumin, and cayenne. Mix thoroughly. Place in an ovenproof dish and cook until vegetables are tender, about 20 minutes. Transfer to a medium-sized sauce pot, adding tomato juice and water. Reduce liquid to one-third of its original volume. Transfer sauce to a blender and purée until smooth. Season with salt and pepper, to taste. Set aside.

PEPPERS

1 1/2 cup whole milk ricotta

1/3 cup Pecorino Romano, grated

3/4 cup Monterey Jack, grated

1 egg

1/2 cup breadcrumbs

2 tablespoons olive oil

2 tablespoons garlic, chopped

1/4 cup onion, finely diced

1/4 cup celery, finely diced

3 tablespoons banana pepper rings

1 teaspoon Italian seasoning

1/8 tablespoon kosher salt

1/8 tablespoon ground black pepper

12 banana peppers, cleaned and deveined

Make stuffing by adding ricotta, Pecorino, and Jack to a large mixing bowl. Add egg and breadcrumbs and mix until thoroughly combined. Set aside.

Heat oil over medium heat in a sauté pan. Sauté garlic, onions, celery, and pepper rings until onions become translucent. Add Italian seasoning, salt, and pepper. Mix thoroughly. Remove from heat and allow mixture to cool to room temperature. Once cooled, add to cheese mixture and combine thoroughly.

Preheat oven to 350 degrees. Neatly and uniformly fill each banana pepper with stuffing. Place in a greased ovenproof dish and cover with foil. Cook for 30 minutes, or until peppers are soft but still a little firm. Serve with warm Red Creole Sauce.

Tortellini in Brodo

KEVIN MCCARTHY, GLOBE MARKET

SERVES 6

3 tablespoons olive oil

1 tablespoon garlic, chopped

1 tablespoon fennel seed

1 teaspoon cracked black pepper

1 teaspoon dry oregano

1/2 teaspoon red pepper flakes

8 cups chicken broth

1 pound cheese tortellini, cooked

1 cup baby spinach, chopped

1/2 cup fresh basil, chopped

Parmesan, freshly grated

Add olive oil to a soup pot, over medium heat. Once hot, slowly add garlic, fennel, black pepper, oregano, and red pepper. Cook for a minute and add the chicken broth. Increase heat and bring to a boil. Reduce heat and add the tortellini. Simmer for another five minutes before adding the spinach and basil. Cook until greens are wilted. Divide into bowls and top with Parmesan.

Black Bean Soup

KRISTA VAN WAGNER, CURLY'S GRILL AND BANQUET CENTER

SERVES 8

1 cup bacon, diced

6 cloves garlic, chopped

1 large onion, diced

1 large carrot, diced

2 celery ribs, diced

4 cups black beans, soaked overnight and drained

8 cups chicken stock

1 tablespoon ground cumin

1/2 teaspoon ground black pepper

1/2 teaspoon crushed red pepper

Salt, to taste

Cheddar, grated (optional)

Sweet onion, minced (optional)

Sour cream (optional)

In a heavy-bottomed stock pot, cook bacon until almost brown. Drain fat. Add garlic and sauté until fragrant. Add remaining vegetables and cook until translucent. Add beans, stock, and seasonings. Cover the pot and bring to a boil. Reduce to a simmer and cook for 60 to 90 minutes, or until beans are tender. Purée soup until creamy in texture. Adjust salt and pepper to taste. Garnish with optional cheese, onion, or sour cream.

Chef Joe George's Basmati Pilaf with Almonds and Raisins

JOE GEORGE, EXECUTIVE CHEF, 20TH CENTURY CLUB

George has been cooking in Western New York restaurants for decades and writing about it for *Buffalo Spree* since 1999. Today he runs the kitchen at the 20th Century Club, one of the oldest private women's clubs in the United States. Located in a stunning building designed by E. B. Green, George's cuisine is as rooted in the classics as the building in which he works.

Basmati Pilaf with Almonds and Raisins

JOE GEORGE, 20TH CENTURY CLUB

SERVES 6

- 2 tablespoons unsalted clarified butter
- 1/2 cup onion, diced
- 1 teaspoon garlic, minced
- 1 teaspoon saffron threads
- 1 teaspoon salt
- 1/4 teaspoon ground black pepper
- 2 cups basmati rice
- 3 cups chicken broth, hot
- 1/4 cup raisins
- 1/4 cup toasted almonds, sliced

Heat the butter in a heavy-bottomed pot. Add the onion and garlic; sauté over medium heat for 5 minutes. Add the saffron, salt, and pepper; sauté another minute. Stir in the rice and hot broth. Cover pot and simmer for 15 minutes. Remove rice from the stove and allow it to rest for 5 minutes. Stir in the raisins and almonds.

Chicken Thighs with Vinegar Peppers

ROCCO'S WOOD FIRED PIZZA

SERVES 6

VINEGAR PEPPERS

1 large red bell pepper

1 large orange bell pepper

1 large yellow bell pepper

2 tablespoons olive oil

6 cloves garlic, minced

1/2 cup red wine vinegar

Salt and pepper, to taste

Cut each of the peppers in half. Remove and discard the stems and seeds. Slice each pepper into 1/2-inch strips. In a sauté pan, heat olive oil and garlic. Add peppers and cook until they begin to soften. Season with salt and pepper. Add vinegar and simmer until liquid is reduced by half.

RELISH

10 cloves garlic, thinly sliced

3 anchovy fillets

1 medium red onion, minced

1 small fennel bulb, minced

2 tablespoons capers

2 tablespoons dried currants, soaked and drained

1 red bell pepper, minced

1 6 ounce can tomato paste

Salt and pepper, to taste

1 tablespoon fresh thyme, stems removed

1 tablespoon fresh rosemary, stems removed

1 cup dry white wine

2 tablespoons red wine vinegar

In a sauté pan over medium heat, cook the garlic and anchovies until fragrant. Add onion and fennel and sauté until tender. Add the capers, currents, red pepper, and cook until pepper begins to soften. Add tomato paste and stir until smooth. Allow relish to caramelize. Add wine, vinegar, and herbs. Cook for 5 minutes until alcohol has burned off and herbs have warmed. Cool.

CHICKEN THIGHS AND SPICE RUB

12 large bone-in chicken thighs

1 tablespoon chili powder

1 tablespoon Spanish paprika

1 tablespoon granulated garlic

1 tablespoon onion powder

1 tablespoon ground fennel seed

1 tablespoon black pepper

2 tablespoons salt

1/4 cup vegetable oil

1/4 cup olive oil

1 jar Italian oil-packed tuna (optional)

1/2 cup fresh flat-leaf parley, chopped (optional)

Preheat oven to 375 degrees. Pat chicken thighs dry. Combine all spices into a small bowl. Mix vegetable oil and olive oil together. Rub thighs with spice rub, and coat lightly with oil. Place on a baking sheet and cook for 30 to 35 minutes.

ASSEMBLE

To serve family style, place chicken thighs on a large platter. Smother with peppers and relish. Garnish with flaked Italian tuna and chopped parsley, if using.

Sweet Potato Bisque

LUIGI ALFANO, THE HOLLOW BISTRO AND BREW

SERVES 10

1/4 cup oil

2 large carrots, chopped

1/2 stalk celery, chopped

1 small onion, chopped

6 large sweet potatoes, skinned and cubed

Water

8 cups heavy whipping cream

3 tablespoons ground nutmeg

1 cup maple syrup

Salt and white pepper, to taste

ROUX

1 tablespoon unsalted butter, cold

1 tablespoon all-purpose flour

Heat oil in a large pot over medium heat. Once hot, add carrots, celery, onion, and sweet potatoes. Sauté for 10 minutes, until onion is translucent and potatoes begins to brown. Add water to cover and bring to a boil for 5 minutes. Reduce heat and simmer until largest potatoes are fork tender. Add the cream and continue to simmer for 25 minutes. Stir in remaining ingredients and purée with a hand blender or in a regular blender. If the soup is too thin, use the roux.

To make the roux, combine the butter with flour and mix thoroughly. Bring the pot back to medium heat. Return the soup to the pot and whisk in the roux. Stirring regularly, cook for another 15 minutes until desired thickness has been reached.

Acorn Squash with Cider Vinegar Sauce

ANDREW NUERNBEREGER, THE ROYCROFT INN

SERVES 4

2 acorn squashes

2 teaspoons unsalted butter

2 teaspoons shallots, minced

4 teaspoons granulated sugar

4 teaspoons cider vinegar

1/2 cup beef stock

1/2 cup chicken stock

Remove the ends from each squash. Clean out seeds. Slice each squash into 1/2-inch rings. Fill a pot with an inch of water and steam squash on high heat for 8 minutes, or until fork tender. Remove rings from water and set aside. Empty any water left in the pot and return to heat. Add the butter. Once it has melted, add the shallots and sauté until translucent. Add sugar, cider vinegar, beef and chicken stock, and reduce by half. Return rings of squash to the pot and cook for 1 minute.

Ricotta Gnocchi with Brown Butter Cream and Wilted Spinach

ADAM GOETZ, CRAVE

SERVES 4

GNOCCHI

1 cup whole milk ricotta cheese

1/2 cup Parmesan, grated

2 eggs

1 teaspoon kosher salt

1 teaspoon ground white pepper

Zest of half a lemon

1 cup all-purpose flour

In a large mixing bowl combine cheeses, eggs, salt, pepper, and lemon zest. Slowly add the flour until a dough forms and the consistency resembles children's play dough. Remove the dough from the bowl and cover with a damp cloth. Lightly dust work surface with flour. Roll the dough into long thin logs, about the thickness of your index finger. Cut logs into 1/2-inch lengths and reserve on a floured baking sheet. Place a large pot of salted water on the stove to boil. Once the water is at a rolling boil, carefully add the gnocchi and cook until they float to the top. Strain.

**BROWN BUTTER CREAM SAUCE
AND WILTED SPINACH**

2 tablespoons unsalted butter

1/2 cup walnut pieces

3 cups fresh baby spinach

1 cup heavy cream

Salt and pepper, to taste

On the stovetop, put butter in a sauté pan over medium heat. Add the cooked gnocchi. Once they begin to brown slightly, add the nuts and spinach. When spinach begins to wilt, add the cream and reduce until sauce thickens to a desired consistency. Season with salt and pepper.

Eggplant Puttanesca

TOM DIANA, SALVATORE'S ITALIAN GARDENS

2 SERVINGS

2 large eggs

1/2 cup milk

1/2 cup Parmesan, grated

1 cup all-purpose flour

1 teaspoon salt

1/2 teaspoon ground black pepper

1 eggplant, cut into lengthwise 1/4-inch slices

1/2 cup vegetable oil

4 slices fresh Mozzarella

2 tablespoons olive oil

1 tablespoon fresh garlic, thinly sliced

2 cups canned diced plum tomatoes with juice

2 teaspoon capers

Salt and pepper, to taste

2 tablespoons fresh basil, chiffonade

2 tablespoons Asiago, grated

Preheat oven to 350 degrees. Whisk together eggs, milk, and Parmesan in a shallow bowl. Set aside. In another shallow dish, combine flour, salt, and pepper. Dredge eggplant in seasoned flour and then in egg batter.

In a large sauté pan over medium heat, add oil. Cook eggplant until it is golden brown. Drain on paper towel and set aside to cool.

Place four slices of eggplant on a cutting board or other flat surface. Top with a slice of Mozzarella. Form into a tight roll. Complete this step with all four eggplant slices. Now repeat by placing the four remaining slices of eggplant on the work surface. Place the existing eggplant-Mozzarella rolls onto the flat eggplant slice. Roll into the eggplant going the opposite direction, making an eggplant bundle with no openings. This creates a seal so that most of the Mozzarella stays inside during the final cooking process. Place the four eggplant-Mozzarella bundles in a greased ovenproof dish. Put in oven and cook 5 to 7 minutes, until Mozzarella begins to melt. Meanwhile, in a sauté pan over medium heat, cook olive oil and garlic until it becomes fragrant. Add tomatoes and capers to the pan and simmer. Season with salt and pepper to taste, add basil and remove from stove.

Remove eggplant from oven. On each plate arrange two pieces of eggplant. Top with plum tomato sauce and Asiago garnish.

Sun's Own No Koksware

KEVIN LIN, OWNER/EXECUTIVE CHEF, SUN RESTAURANT
Born and raised in Burma, Lin spent years traveling and touring his homeland and working as a sous chef in Tokyo. In 1996 he moved to the United States, and a few years later purchased a sushi franchise in a Pennsylvania supermarket. What soon followed was ownership of a similar franchise in supermarkets throughout Buffalo. In 2001, Lin's passion for food led him to open Sun.
What is your favorite aspect of being a chef?
"Creating new dishes."

Own No Koksware

KEVIN LIN, SUN RESTAURANT

SERVES 10

4 tablespoons vegetable
    oil

2 tablespoons fresh ginger,
    grated

2 teaspoons paprika

2 teaspoons turmeric

4 cups onion, diced

3 pounds chicken thighs,
    deboned, skin removed,
    cut into 1/2-inch cubes

3 cups water

1 cup chickpea flour, plus 3
    tablespoons water

3/4 cup granulated sugar

2 teaspoons salt

1/3 cup fish sauce

1 13 1/2 ounce can
    coconut milk

2 pounds lo mein noodles,
    cooked

10 hard boiled eggs,
    halved

6 ounces flat, crispy rice
    noodles

1 cup fresh cilantro,
    chopped

3 limes, halved

Heat vegetable oil in a large Dutch oven. Add ginger, paprika, and turmeric. Once warm and fragrant, add onion and chicken. Cook for 10 minutes, stirring occasionally. Add water to cover and bring to a boil.

In a small dish, create a slurry by whisking chickpea flour with the 3 tablespoons of water.

Add the slurry to the soup and stir thoroughly. Cover and cook until chicken is cooked through. Add sugar, salt, fish sauce, and coconut milk and cook for another ten minutes, stirring occasionally.

To serve, place cooked noodles and hard boiled eggs in the center of each large soup bowl. Spoon broth over top. Garnish with crispy noodles, cilantro, and a squeeze of fresh lime.

Haddock Francais

TODD POSCH, GLEN PARK TAVERN

SERVES 4

3 eggs
3/4 cup Parmesan, grated
1/2 cup parsley, chopped
2 tablespoons unsalted butter
4 pieces haddock fillet (or other whitefish)
3/4 cup all-purpose flour
1 teaspoon garlic, chopped
1 lemon, juiced
1/4 cup dry white wine
Salt and pepper, to taste

Whisk together eggs, cheese, and parsley in a shallow dish. Coat the fillets in the egg mixture and set aside, discarding any unused batter. Heat butter in a sauté pan on the stovetop over medium-high heat. Add the fish fillets to pan and cook for 2 minutes until one side is golden brown. Turn the fish over and add the garlic. Cook until garlic becomes fragrant. Add the lemon juice. Remove from heat and add the wine. Return to heat and cook until alcohol has burnt off. Simmer until the fillets are white and flaky. Season with salt and pepper.

Chicken Scallopini

MARK SCIORTINO,
MARCO'S ITALIAN RESTAURANT

SERVES 4

8 4-ounce boneless chicken breasts, pounded thin
1 3/4 cups olive oil
1 cup all-purpose flour
4 thin slices prosciutto
8 slices fresh Mozzarella
2 cloves garlic, chopped
1/2 small red onion, thinly sliced
3/4 cup Marsala wine
1 cup tomatoes, chopped
1/4 teaspoon dry oregano
Salt and pepper, to taste

Preheat oven to 375 degrees.

On the stovetop, heat an ovenproof sauté pan over medium heat. Add 1 and 1/2 cups of the oil. While oil is warming, dredge the chicken in flour until lightly coated. Add to the pan and begin cooking. When the chicken develops a golden crust on one side, flip and continue to cook on the other. Once both sides are golden brown and each fillet has reached an internal temperature of 160 degrees, place a slice of prosciutto and two slices of Mozzarella on top of each piece of chicken. Remove the pan from the stovetop and place in the oven until the cheese has melted.

In a separate pan, sauté the garlic and onion in remaining oil. Add the wine with care, as the alcohol may flame. Reduce the liquid for 30 seconds and add tomatoes. Bring the mixture to a quick boil. Season with oregano, salt, and pepper. To serve, remove chicken from the oven and plate, topping each piece with the tomato pan sauce.

Pork Osso Buco with Sweet Potato Gnocchi

JACOB ZACHOW, DELLA TERRA RESTAURANT

SERVES 6

SWEET POTATO GNOCCHI

- 1 cup sweet potatoes, cooked and mashed
- 1/3 cup whole milk ricotta
- 1 tablespoon Parmesan, grated
- 1/2 tablespoon brown sugar
- 1/2 teaspoon cinnamon
- 3/4 teaspoon salt
- 1/4 teaspoon ground black pepper
- 1 cup all-purpose flour

In a mixing bowl, combine sweet potatoes, ricotta, Parmesan, sugar, cinnamon, salt, and pepper. Fold gently until thoroughly combined. Slowly add the flour, mixing gently until completely incorporated. Turn dough out onto a floured board and divide into smaller, manageable batches. Rolling the dough between your palms and the board, form each piece into a rope about 1-inch in diameter. Sprinkle with flour as you work. Cut each rope into 1-inch pieces and transfer pasta to a baking sheet that is parchment-lined or lightly floured. Bring a large pot of salted water to boil. Working in batches,cook gnocchi until tender, about 5 minutes. Return gnocchi to the baking sheet and cool. When the pork is done and the braising liquid is reducing (as outlined in the next step), sauté the desired amount of gnocchi in hot butter until the outsides begin to turn crispy and brown, but the inside of each gnocchi is still soft.

PORK OSSO BUCO

- 6 12–16 ounce pork shanks
- 2 tablespoons olive oil
- Salt and pepper, to taste
- 1/2 onion, chopped
- 1 carrot, chopped
- 1 parsnip, chopped
- 1 bottle Madeira wine
- 2 gallons pork or beef stock
- 2 sprigs fresh oregano, stems removed
- 1/4 cup tomato paste
- 1/2 tablespoon juniper berries

Rub oil, salt, and pepper into the shanks. In a large Dutch oven, sear the shanks over high heat, achieving a golden brown crust on all sides. Remove from pan and set aside.

In the same pan, cook the onion, carrot, and parsnip until they are about half done. Add Madeira and deglaze the pan. Add beef stock, oregano, paste, and juniper. Return the pork shanks to the pan and cook on a slow simmer for at least 3 hours. To determine doneness, look for the meat to fall from the bone. Remove the pork and set aside. Strain the cooking liquid. Return it to the pan and reduce by half.

ASSEMBLE

Serve family style by placing the pork in the center of a large pasta bowl or platter. Add the pan-fried gnocchi and ladle sauce over the top.

Spicy Pork Meatballs with Swiss Chard

CARMELO RAIMONDI, CARMELO'S

SERVES 8

MEATBALLS

2 tablespoon olive oil

1 onion, minced

5 cloves garlic, minced

1 pound ground pork

1 tablespoon fresh basil, chopped

2 tablespoons crushed red pepper

3 tablespoons Parmesan, grated

2 large eggs, lightly beaten

1/4 cup breadcrumbs

Coarse salt and freshly ground pepper

3 shallots, minced

2 plum tomatoes, chopped

1/2 cup white wine

8 cups chicken stock

8 sprigs fresh thyme, stems removed

Preheat oven to 425 degrees. Heat 1 tablespoon of the olive oil in a large skillet over medium heat. Add the onion and a little more than half of the garlic. Cook and stir until onions become translucent, about 5 minutes. Remove from heat and let cool.

In a large mixing bowl combine ground pork, cooled garlic and onion mixture, basil, red pepper, Parmesan, eggs, and breadcrumbs. Season with salt and pepper. Combine thoroughly using clean, bare hands. Form into 1 and 1/2-inch meatballs. Place meatballs on a baking sheet and cook in the oven for 10 minutes.

On the stovetop, heat the remaining oil in a large saucepan over medium heat. Add remaining garlic, shallots, and tomatoes. Cook, stirring occasionally, for 2 minutes. Add wine and cook until liquid is reduced by half, about 4 minutes. Add stock and thyme and simmer for about 20 minutes. Strain the cooking sauce through a fine-mesh strainer set over another large saucepan. Discard solids. Place meatballs in the sauce and cover. Simmer over medium heat until cooked through, about 30 minutes.

BRAISED CHARD

1 head of Swiss chard,
  leaves and stalks
  separated
1/4 cup canola oil
1 anchovy fillet
2 cloves garlic, minced
Pinch crushed red
  pepper
Salt and pepper, to taste

Bring 6 cups of salted water
to a boil. Cook the chard
stalks until they begin
to grow tender. Add the
leaves, cooking for just a
minute or two. Strain the
chard, reserving cooking
liquid. Add chard to ice
water bath and let soak
until cool. Use your hands
to wring the leaves out
thoroughly. Set aside.
Heat oil in a sauté pan
over medium heat. Sauté
anchovy until dissolved.
Add garlic and red pepper
flakes. Cook until fragrant.
Add 1/2 cup of the reserved
chard cooking water and
the greens and cook until
water is evaporated. Add
salt and pepper to taste.

CRISPY PARMIGIANO

3/4 cup Parmesan, grated
Freshly ground black
  pepper
Extra virgin olive oil

Preheat oven to 300
degrees. Using a
tablespoon, place cheese
in mounds onto a nonstick
silicone pad or parchment
paper-lined baking sheet.
Flatten mounds with the
back of a spoon, making
sure cheese mounds are at
least 4 inches apart. Season
with pepper. Bake on the
middle rack of the oven
for 5 to 6 minutes, or until
golden brown.

ASSEMBLE

Place 3 to 4 meatballs
in each bowl. Top with
chard. Pool meatball
cooking sauce around the
meatballs. Top with crispy
Parmesan and dribble with
extra virgin olive oil.

BBQ Pulled Pork with Root Vegetable Hash, Poached Egg and Chive Aioli

KEITH DULAK, TRATTORIA AROMA

SERVES 4

PORK

- 4–6 pound pork shoulder, bone in
- 2 liters of cola
- 2 cups red wine vinegar
- 8 cups chicken stock
- 1 bulb garlic, cloves separated and peeled
- 2 carrots, peeled and chopped
- 1 stalk celery, chopped

Preheat oven to 375.
Heat a large, deep roasting pan on the stove top. Sear the pork shoulder on all sides until browned. Add cola, vinegar, stock, garlic, carrots, and celery. Bring to a slow boil. Remove from heat, cover and place in oven. Cook for 3 to 4 hours, checking after 2 hours for doneness. Pork should easily fall off the bone when pressed.

CHIVE AIOLI

- 3 eggs
- 1 bunch chives, chopped
- 2 cups vegetable oil
- 3 tablespoons white vinegar
- Salt and pepper, to taste

Fill a sauce pan with water and bring to boil. Add the eggs and boil for 10 to 15 seconds to sanitize outer shell thoroughly. Put eggs under cold water to cool completely. Crack eggs into a food processor. Add the chives and turn the processor on low. Slowly add the oil until mixture begins to thicken. Add the vinegar and continue to pulse mixture to fully incorporate. Aioli should resemble loose mayonnaise. Season and set aside.

ROOT VEGETABLE HASH

- 2 cups rutabaga, grated
- 2 cups parsnip, grated
- 2 cups carrot, grated
- 2 cups beets, grated
- 1 egg
- 1/4 cup all-purpose flour
- Salt and pepper, to taste
- 3 tablespoons olive oil

Combine grated root vegetables in a large bowl. Using a strainer or your hands, squeeze as much liquid as possible from mixture. Add the egg and the flour to the vegetable mixture. Season with salt and pepper. Cover and refrigerate until pork is nearly done. When pork is nearing readiness, add olive oil to a hot sauté pan. Form vegetable mixture into patties and carefully add to hot pan. Brown on both sides, cooking thoroughly. Remove and drain on paper towels. Cover with tented aluminum foil to hold heat, if necessary.

ASSEMBLE

- 4 eggs, poached

Poach eggs. See instructions on page 115. Once the pork has finished braising, remove it from pan and cover it with foil. Strain liquid into a pot and reduce by half on the stovetop. Season.
When pork is cool enough to handle, begin to shred pork and set in bowl with some of the warm braising liquid.
To serve, place a root vegetable cake on each plate. Top each cake with pulled pork, a poached egg, and a garnish of aioli.

Chubby Hubby Brownie

**TRISH MULLANEY,
DESSERT DELI GOURMET BAKERY AND CAFE**

YIELDS 1 DOZEN

5 cups milk chocolate chips

1 cup white chocolate chips

1 1/2 cups pecans, chopped

2 cups walnuts, chopped

1/2 pound unsweetened chocolate

2 tablespoons vanilla extract

1 pound unsalted butter, room temperature

4 cups brown sugar

8 eggs

3 cups all-purpose flour

Preheat oven to 325 degrees. In a medium mixing bowl, combine chips, pecans, and walnuts. Set aside.

Heat unsweetened chocolate in a double boiler until melted. Remove from heat and stir in vanilla. Set aside.

In a large mixing bowl, cream sugar and butter. Beat in eggs one at a time. Beat in melted chocolate. Add flour and mix just until combined. Fold in half the chip and nut mixture. Spread mixture into a greased rectangular baking pan. Sprinkle remaining chips and nuts on top of batter. Press slightly with hand to secure them. Bake 20 to 30 minutes, until a cake tester can be inserted and removed cleanly. Be careful not to overbake. Cool before cutting.

Aviation Creme Brulee

KARL WYANT, VERA

SERVES 10

8 egg yolks

1 1/2 cups granulated
 sugar

1/2 cup gin

1/4 cup lemon juice

1/8 cup Luxardo liqueur

1/8 cup Creme de Violette

4 cups heavy cream

Preheat oven to 325 degrees. In a large mixing bowl, whisk yolks and 1 cup of the sugar until combined. Set aside. In a small saucepan, heat gin, juice, liqueur, Creme de Violette, and 1/4 cup of the sugar. Cook over low heat until the liquid is reduced by half, being attentive, because the alcohol may flame once heated. Set aside.

In a medium saucepan over medium heat, warm the cream slowly, stirring until it comes to a simmer. Remove from heat. Slowly add the cream, one cup at a time, to yolks and sugar, whisking constantly and attentively. Once combined, add the gin mixture, whisking again until thoroughly combined. Pour mixture into ten 5- to 6-ounce ramekins. Bake in a water bath for approximately 45 minutes, or until the creme is set. Remove from oven and refrigerate until cool.

To serve, sprinkle remaining sugar on top and brown with a kitchen torch, or very briefly under a hot broiler.

Aunt Ronnie's Zucchini Bread

MELISSA GARDNER, FIVE POINTS BAKERY

YIELDS 1 LOAF

- 1 1/2 cups zucchini, grated
- 1 1/4 cups organic raw sugar
- 1/3 cup cold pressed sunflower oil
- 2 large eggs, slightly beaten
- 2 cups whole grain pastry flour
- 1 teaspoon baking soda
- 1 teaspoon sea salt
- 1/4 teaspoon baking powder
- 1/2 teaspoon cinnamon
- 1/4 teaspoon nutmeg
- 1/3 cup toasted walnuts, chopped
- 1/3 cup 60% dark chocolate chips

Preheat oven to 350 degrees. Combine zucchini, sugar, oil, and eggs in a large bowl. Mix with a wooden spoon until combined. In a separate bowl combine flour, soda, salt, baking powder, cinnamon, and nutmeg until thoroughly combined. Add chips and walnuts into the flour mixture (this will prevent them from sinking to the bottom). Add flour mixture to the bowl of zucchini, sugar, and egg, and mix thoroughly. Spoon dough into a lightly greased loaf pan. Place in the oven on the top rack and bake approximately 1 hour, or until a cake tester emerges clean. Cool before slicing.

Grandma Tomaselli's German Apple Cake

SHERRY NUGENT, LA TEE DA CAFE

YIELDS ONE 8" CAKE

- 2 cups all-purpose flour
- 1 3/4 cups granulated sugar
- 1 teaspoon baking soda
- 1/2 teaspoon salt
- 3 teaspoons cinnamon
- 3 large eggs
- 1 cup vegetable oil
- 1 tablespoon vanilla
- 1 cup walnuts, chopped
- 1 cup raisins
- 2 1/2 cups apples, peeled and sliced

Preheat oven to 350 degrees. Sift dry ingredients into a mixing bowl. In a separate bowl, beat eggs and oil together until foamy and light. Add vanilla, raisins, and apples and mix. Now add the sifted dry ingredients to the wet, and mix thoroughly. Pour the thick batter into an ungreased 8-inch x 8-inch glass cake pan. Bake for 40 to 45 minutes or until a cake tester emerges clean.

Using This Cookbook: Standard Techniques

BLANCHING VEGETABLES AND COOKING PASTA

On any occasion when food is cooked, seasoning is required. Whether you are blanching fresh vegetables or boiling a pot of spaghetti, the water should be seasoned. Adding salt during cooking actually melds the flavor with the food, which is always better than simply sprinkling it on top. We recommend using kosher salt or sea salt, and adding enough that the cooking water tastes as salty as the sea. For example, a 4-quart pot of water will require at least 3 tablespoons of salt. This may seem like a lot, but the ingredient will only absorb a small amount of salt. Think of it as seasoning from the inside out.

BREADING AND BATTERING

Several recipes in this book require ingredients to be breaded or battered. We've included each chef's specific instructions within each recipe, but thought we would also offer some tips and tricks for carrying this process out at home as efficiently as possible.

We always recommend that you think like a chef and set up a breading/battering station, of sorts, using shallow dishes (like pie plates or pasta bowls) as the vessel for your breading/battering ingredients.

A 3-step process is the most traditional. It typically requires seasoned flour, some form of liquid—usually beaten eggs or buttermilk—and a third coating, which can be flour, breadcrumbs, or anything else that will crisp during cooking. Using shallow dishes, set the called for breading/battering ingredients up in order, with a plate or baking sheet at the end for holding the completed breaded/battered ingredients.

The first coating of flour should be seasoned, so add salt and white pepper to the flour, allowing that seasoning to have direct contact with the ingredient it is coating. The second step, which can include dipping in buttermilk or egg, will be greatly aided by having the first flour coating as a base. In the instance of egg wash, add a little water and be sure to beat the eggs well for smooth, even coverage. The final coating of breadcrumbs or flour should also be seasoned. Once you've completed the third step of breading/battering, use your hand to pat and gently press the coating to the ingredient.

POACHING EGGS

Many recipes in this book call for the addition of a poached egg. It's a very popular way to add protein and richness to a dish, and, once you've mastered the ability to make them, you'll find it easy enough to do.

The fresher the egg is, the easier it is to poach. We recommend cooking no more than 4 poached eggs in a pan at one time, but if you've never poached an egg before, you'll want to practice with one at a time until you're conformable.

You will need a slotted spoon, white vinegar, salt, a plate with a paper towel on it, and small bowls or ramekins for each of the eggs you wish to cook. To begin, pour 1 tablespoon of white vinegar into each of the ramekins. Next, crack each of the eggs to be poached into their own ramekin. On the stovetop, bring 2 inches of water to boil in a saucepan. Add a large pinch of salt for seasoning. Using the slotted spoon, swirl the cooking water vigorously, creating a vortex in the center of the pan. Carefully slip one egg and its vinegar into the center of the vortex. Continue to stir the water in the same motion without touching the egg. This should cause the white of the egg to wrap itself around the yolk. As soon as the water returns to a boil, reduce the heat to medium and cook the egg gently, swirling the water, for approximately 2 minutes. Use the slotted spoon to remove the egg from the water. Place egg on paper towels and gently blot. Season with salt and pepper before serving.

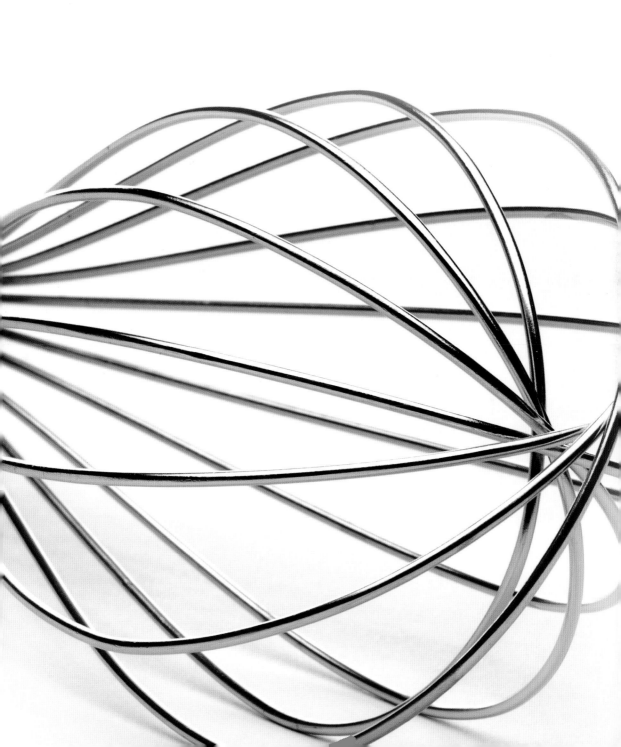

INDEX
BY CHEF

INDEX

BY RESTAURANT

INDEX
BY MAIN INGREDIENTS